Teacher's
MANUAL

to

Roll of Thunder, Hear My Cry

By Ann Maouyo

Talent Development Secondary
Center for Social Organization of Schools
Johns Hopkins University
Baltimore

© 2014 by Johns Hopkins Talent Development, All Rights Reserved
These materials were developed by the Talent Development Secondary Program of
The Center for Social Organization of Schools
The Johns Hopkins University, C.S.O.S., 2701 N. Charles Street, Suite 300, Baltimore, Maryland 21218
Permission is granted to copy and distribute reproducible pages only for classroom use. Other reproductions without permission are prohibited.
Cover photo: http://www.flickr.com/photos/laffy4k/260407952/ cca 2.0

Table of Contents

To the Teacher	i
Planning and preparation	1
Chapters 1 - 3	4
Chapters 4 - 6	22
Chapters 7 - 8	36
Chapters 9 - 12	49
Character Portrait transparency master	63
Selection Review reproducibles	65
Literature Test reproducibles	73
Vocabulary Test reproducibles	81

TALENT DEVELOPMENT SECONDARY (TDS)
ENGLISH LANGUAGE ARTS DIVISION
MISSION STATEMENT

RESPONDING TO THE CHANGING NATURE OF LITERACY BY PROVIDING STUDENTS WITH SKILLS THAT WILL ENDURE BEYOND THE CLASSROOM

Student Team Literature Discussion Guides are designed to support teachers with organizing literacy instruction to respond to the needs of diverse student populations while striving to meet the growing instructional demands of state and district college- and career-readiness standards.

Using whole-class structures, peer discussion, and teacher modeling, this instructional framework affords students regular opportunities to engage in oral language, critical analysis and exploration of information extending to real world applications. Students intuitively deepen understanding of content and develop their inferring and evidence-gathering skills through ongoing exposure to inductive learning, a powerful strategy underlying higher-order thinking and 21st century skills. Teachers routinely facilitate small-group and whole-class discussions to help students apply academic language and develop new insights and perspectives as they read various types of authentic texts. Teachers are also encouraged and equipped to use a variety of informational texts in conjunction with literary works, and to provide students with the skills they need to comprehend these increasingly complex texts. Through reading and writing for different purposes and from multiple perspectives, students move toward the self-regulated learning and independent thinking required to function in today's society.

In the midst of the flow of information surrounding adolescent literacy, we recognize the significant role that motivation plays in the lives of adolescent learners. The instructional design and materials used in the TDS program enable students to exercise mental processes needed to comprehend, communicate, reason, evaluate, and persevere. Students take ownership of learning experiences and make choices within a responsive, student-centered classroom environment.

With the growing demands of the 21st century, the TDS ELA Discussion Guides offer flexibility and guidance to teachers who seek specific focus and clarity when planning instruction. Teachers are able to build instructional modules around core reading selections using existing approaches and activities contained in the Discussion Guides. This approach helps establish historical and factual connections, and addresses specific assessments, standards and skills in the context of teaching the core reading selections. Using this method to planning and teaching literacy, classroom teachers and TDS instructional support staff can effectively collaborate around core approaches to promote achievement for all students in the 21st century.

To the Teacher

This Teacher's Manual is part of a research-based, cooperative approach to teaching literature developed by the Talent Development Secondary Program at the Johns Hopkins University. This approach, called Student Team Literature, strengthens students' thinking, reading, writing, and social skills. In Student Team Literature, students read quality books and work in learning teams using *Student Discussion Guides* that lead them to become critical thinkers, expand their working vocabularies, and broaden their knowledge of the writer's craft. Guides are available to support study of over 70 novels, biographies, and short story and poetry collections. Students read the literature and work through a Student Discussion Guide using a weekly cycle of instruction.

Each Student Discussion Guide includes the following components:

- **Vocabulary Lists** expose students to terms they need to know in order to understand what they are reading.

- **Starred High Frequency Words** are those that students acquire for their working vocabularies, as they occur often in many contexts. Students learn to use these words in meaningful sentences that include context clues to show understanding of the new words.

- **Writer's Craft Boxes** provide information about aspects of the writer's craft (e.g., flashbacks, figurative language) that students encounter in the literature. Craft Boxes can be used as the basis for mini-lessons.

- **Questions** and **Graphic Organizers** lead students to analyze the literature, organize information, and better understand the writer's message.

- **Make a Prediction** and **What If? Boxes** lead students to establish expectations about what will come next in their reading.

- **Selection Review** questions and answers are used by pairs of students to prepare for literature tests.

- **Literature-related Writing** suggestions lead students to respond to literature and try various forms of writing.

- **Extension Activities** give students opportunities to express themselves in response to the text through art, drama, research, and other activities.

- **So, You Want to Read More...** suggests books for independent reading that match the one students have read in theme, genre, or topic.

- **About the Author** provides biographical information, as well as listing some of the writer's other works.

In addition to these sections, each Teacher's Manual also includes:

- a **Summary** of the book or literary work

- a **Building Background** section with suggestions for preparing students to read the literary work

- a **Preview/Predict/Purpose** section with questions that lead students to establish expectations before beginning to read

- **Guided Discussion** questions and suggestions for whole-class discussions

- **Listening Comprehension/Read Aloud Connections** identifying relevant literary elements and devices and listing short works that include these features, which teachers can use to prepare and present *Listening Comprehension* lessons (a teacher read-aloud/think-aloud activity that serves as a companion to Student Team Literature)

These materials can be used within or outside the context of the Student Team Literature program, although we believe teachers who have been trained in the program make the best use of them. (Please see below for teacher training contact information.)

About the Literature

The most effective motivation for adolescent readers lies in the relevance of the literature they are presented. Poor or reluctant readers are particularly in need of relevance in the written word. They need to see themselves in the pages they turn.

Today's adolescents are fortunate; never have they had so much quality literature available that reflects their experiences, their problems, and their cultures. The driving force behind Student Team Literature is making accessible the best of middle grades literature. Discussion Guides have been written for a wide variety of literary works at every readability level, from high interest/low readability selections to classic literature used in middle grades English language arts instruction for over twenty-five years.

Talent Development Secondary Program

The Weekly Instruction Cycle

Discussion Guides enable teachers to lead learning teams through literary works in a cycle of activities that includes **direct instruction**, **team practice and discussion**, and **individual assessment**. After careful preliminary vocabulary instruction, students: (1) read a selected text portion silently; (2) complete (optional) Partner Reading, which gives poor readers and second language learners additional practice to build fluency by reading excerpts aloud; (3) discuss with their partners possible responses to questions and activities in Student Discussion Guides; and, (4) write individual responses to the questions and activities.

Discussion Guides and Cooperative Learning

Discussion Guides are designed to be used in the classroom in the context of cooperative learning. Cooperative learning requires students to learn and exercise many social and academic skills, beginning with the most basic, such as active listening and staying on task. For that reason, introducing students (and teachers, during professional development) to Student Team Literature typically involves direct instruction in relevant skills. The teacher determines the skills to be taught (one at a time), the order in which they will be introduced, and students' readiness to add new skills. Instruction includes discussion of the skill and its importance; completion of a T-chart to show what the skill looks and sounds like (making abstract social skills more concrete for students); and modeling and role-playing use of the skill. As students apply the skills in daily classroom activities, teachers monitor and reinforce their use. Students gradually internalize the skills, creating a cooperative learning climate that has an important positive impact on classroom management and academic achievement.

Assessment

Three assessment tools are available to teachers who use Student Team Literature guides. Each week, after quizzing each other in a process called "Selection Review," students take **literature tests** that require short constructed responses. **Vocabulary tests** assess students' ability to compose meaningful sentences using the high frequency words they have studied in the context of the literature. These Selection Reviews, literature tests, and vocabulary tests are provided on reproducible pages at the end of each Teacher's Manual. In addition, students can practice their standardized test taking skills in relation to the literary work they have studied by taking Standardized Reading Practice Tests that are similar in format to the standardized tests used in school districts throughout the country. Standardized Reading Practice Tests must be ordered separately.

Ordering information

The Talent Development Secondary program offers Teacher's Manuals, Student Discussion Guides, and a Standardized Reading Practice Test booklet including reproducible assessment pages.

- To place an order, call 410-516-4339 or email tds@jhu.edu. The complete Talent Development Secondary materials catalog is available online on our website (see below).

- For teacher training or more on our English language arts, math, science, or social studies programs, contact Maria Waltemeyer at 410-516-2247 or mwaltemeyer@jhu.edu

- Also visit our website at
    www.talentdevelopmentsecondary.com/curriculum

Roll of Thunder, Hear My Cry

By Mildred Taylor

TEACHER'S MANUAL

Suggested length of time to be spent on this book: 4 weeks

Summary

Roll of Thunder, Hear My Cry is the story of the Logans, a strong, proud black Mississippi family determined to maintain their dignity and hold on to their land despite the hardships of the Depression and the humiliating realities of deeply entrenched racism. The story is told from the perspective of nine-year-old Cassie, for whom the year is one of increasingly grim discoveries about the place assigned to her as an African-American. Cassie and her brothers are regularly sprayed with dust or mud by the white children's school bus as they walk for an hour to the black school where their mother teaches seventh grade. The children receive old, battered hand-me-down books. Cassie and her brothers go to town and are infuriated when a shopkeeper keeps them waiting for nearly an hour while he serves his white customers.

Although Cassie's parents are proud people who share her indignation, they are also realists, thoughtfully looking for ways to stand up to injustice without bringing destruction on the family. They caution the children against frequenting the Wallace store because its owners are suspected lynchers who take pleasure in corrupting African-American young people. Cassie's parents, with the help of Mr. Jamison, a compassionate white lawyer, organize their sharecropping neighbors to boycott the Wallaces, angering local white supremacy advocates. Harlan Granger, their land-greedy neighbor, hopes to seize this opportunity to have the Logans' mortgage foreclosed. Soon Mama loses her teaching job, and Daddy's leg is broken in a night attack. Meanwhile, T.J., a shiftless, dishonest neighbor boy, begins to associate with the Simms, two older white teenagers, little realizing that they are setting him up. The story comes to a head when the Simms involve T.J. in a robbery. One of the intended victims is fatally hurt, and a lynching party comes after T.J. Only Daddy's quick thinking and stoic determination can stop the mob violence and avert yet another tragedy.

About The Author

Mildred Taylor was born in Jackson, Mississippi, but grew up in Toledo, Ohio. Her connection to the South remained strong, however, through the family history she heard from her father and through yearly visits to her relatives who still lived there. While she was still in high school, Ms. Taylor wished that her schoolbooks depicted the strong, heroic African-American characters she had come to know. She was determined to write their stories down some day, although it was many years before her dream would become a reality. After graduating from the University of Toledo, she spent two years working with the Peace Corps in Ethiopia. When she returned to the United States, she studied journalism at the University

(cont. on page 2)

About The Author (cont.)

of Colorado, where she helped to create a black studies curriculum. Later, Ms. Taylor moved to Los Angeles, where she worked during the day and wrote books at night. She has one daughter and presently lives in Colorado. *Roll of Thunder, Hear My Cry* is the first book of a trilogy, which also includes *Let the Circle Be Unbroken* and *The Road to Memphis*. Ms. Taylor's other books include *The Song of the Trees* and *The Well: David's Story* (also about the Logan family), and *The Gold Cadillac*.

Building Background

It is important to introduce *Roll of Thunder, Hear My Cry* in relation to its context. Explain to students that at the time this story takes place, many white people in the South were still bitter about the Civil War and the economic devastation that occurred in its aftermath. Meanwhile, the experience of slavery was still not far from the memory of older African Americans. The institution of sharecropping is an important element in the setting of this book. Sharecroppers were poor families (both white and black) who lived on and farmed portions of large farms and plantations. In return for the opportunity to make their living in this way, sharecroppers were required to give a set proportion of their crops (often as much as 50%) to the landowner. Sharecroppers could be evicted at any time and were almost entirely under the power of the landowners, to such an extent that for many the experience was just barely better than slavery. The economically vulnerable sharecroppers felt especially keenly the widespread hardships associated with the Depression. White sharecroppers, far from feeling any sense of solidarity with their African-American neighbors, were often particularly anxious to emphasize their supposed racial superiority. A few whites did have the courage to oppose the prevalent patterns of prejudice and discrimination, and students should be encouraged to take note of the individuals, both black and white, who stand out in this book for their sense of compassion, justice, and common humanity. Also point out to students that the Civil Rights movement of the 1950s and 60s arose in reaction to the types of outrageous injustice described in this book. You may wish to invite students to compare and contrast relationships between blacks and whites in the 1930s and today.

Have students find Mississippi on a map. Point out Memphis, Tennessee; the Delta region; and Louisiana. The story takes place in "Spokane County," a fictional county not too far from Vicksburg.

Listening Comprehension/Read Aloud Connections

Characterization is an essential element of this novel. To focus on characterization, read Alice Walker's *To Hell With Dying,* or Patricia Polacco's *Chicken Sunday*, *My Ol' Man*, or *My Rotten Red-Headed Older Brother*.

TEACHER'S MANUAL
Planning and Preparation

So, You Want To Read More

If you enjoyed *Roll of Thunder, Hear My Cry*, you might enjoy reading other books about young African Americans caught up in the historic struggle for dignity and justice, such as *The Watsons Go to Birmingham, 1963*, by Christopher Paul Curtis. You might also enjoy other stories about African-Americans who draw strength from their families to face difficult situations, such as Virginia Hamilton's *M. C. Higgins the Great*, Alice Mead's *Junebug and the Reverend*, Angela Johnson's *Heaven*, or Walter Dean Myers' *The Glory Field*. *Leon's Story*, by Leon Walter Tillage, is the memoir of a real person who attended school in the segregated South during the Depression and had experiences similar to those described in *Roll of Thunder, Hear My Cry*.

Roll of Thunder, Hear My Cry is an example of **historical fiction** written from the **first-person point of view**. Other examples of this genre are Tony Johnston's *The Wagon* and Polacco's *Pink and Say*. The novel's **setting** is a crucial element; to focus on setting, read Jane Kurtz' *Faraway Home*.

Dialect and **foreshadowing** are features of this novel. To focus on dialect, read Patricia McKissack's *Flossie and the Fox*, Kate Duke's *Aunt Isabel Tells a Good One*, or Ezra Jack Keats' *John Henry*. Examples of foreshadowing are found in "Bedtime for Garth Pig," from Mary Rayner's *Mrs. Pig Gets Cross and Other Stories*, Judi Barrett's *Cloudy With a Chance of Meatballs*, and Chris Van Allsburg's *Jumanji*.

Basic **plot elements**, such as **conflict**, **complication**, **climax**, and **denouement**, are very evident in the novel. To study these elements, read Bernard Waber's *Ira Sleeps Over*, William Hooks' *The Moss Gown*, or Steven Kellogg's *Ralph's Secret Weapon*.

Preview/ Predict/ Purpose

Have students **preview** the book by reading the back cover and looking at the cover illustration and the frontispiece (the illustration facing the title page.) Ask students to guess who the people pictured might be, and what will happen to them in the book. Ask them to guess what the title might mean.

Ask students to **predict** why the Logans might have to fight for their land, and what strategies they might use.

Have students set a **purpose** for reading. They may want to learn more about the life of Southern African Americans during the Depression. They might want to enjoy getting to know the members of a proud and courageous family. They may want to compare their own reaction to injustice and peer pressure with the reactions of the young people in the story.

Talent Development Secondary Program

Discussion Guide #1

Chapters 1–3 (pages 1-68)

Write the starred words on the **VOCABULARY LIST** on the next page and their definitions on chart paper or sentence strips that will remain posted throughout the time that students work on the Discussion Guide.

Prepare a **Vocabulary Prediction Chart** (see illustration below) for students to complete after you have introduced the reading selection and the **VOCABULARY LIST**, and before they have begun to read. The chart contains categories into which starred words from the list are to be placed. Students predict how each starred word relates to the reading selection, or if it is impossible to predict its relationship. Categories can be adjusted according to the type of literature being read.

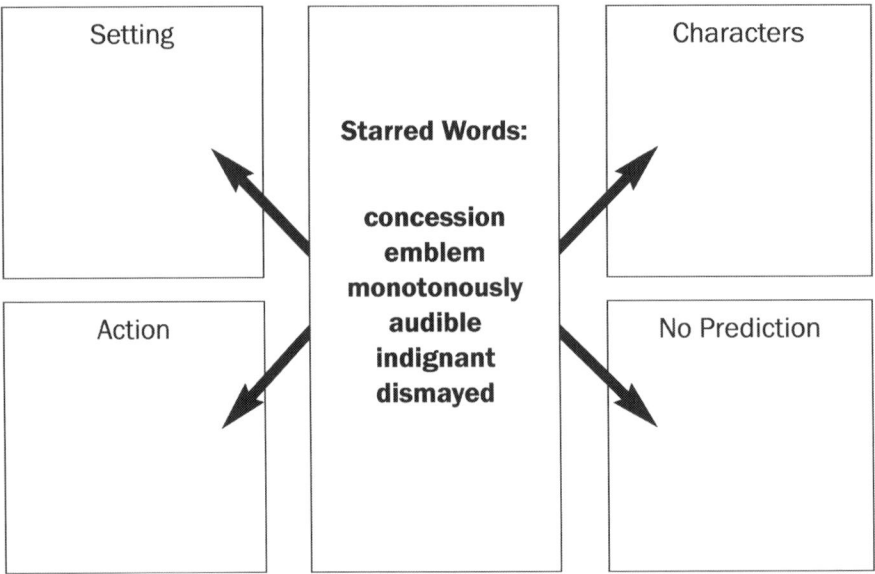

First, read aloud the list of words in the order in which they appear. Second, reread the words and have students repeat each one after you. Third, ask students if they know the definitions of any of the words. Confirm correct definitions, or, in the case of multiple meaning words, identify definitions that match the context in which the words are used in the story. Next, ask students if they recognize parts of unfamiliar words. If students' decoding skills are below level, stress at this time the sounds of syllables — especially in starred words. In all cases, use this time to focus on identifying the meanings of any prefixes, suffixes or roots that are contained in unfamiliar words, and lead students to formulate definitions based upon the meanings of their parts. Finally, provide definitions for any words that remain undefined. **(Definitions of starred words are in the glossaries that follow the Vocabulary Lists. Definitions are *not* provided for the other words in the Vocabulary Lists.)**

Reread the list in random order and have students repeat each word after you. Then point to the words in random order and have the students pronounce each one without your assistance. Return to any words that students have difficulty pronouncing until they can pronounce them correctly. **This process will be repeated each day that students are working on a particular Discussion Guide, so if students still have difficulty pronouncing some of the words, they will have other opportunities for practice and correction**.

Next, lead students in completing the **Vocabulary Prediction Chart.** The importance of this activity lies in encouraging students to make logical connections between what they have been told about the reading selection and specific vocabulary words. **Being correct about predictions is not important; the thought process required to make predictions is**.

The graphic organizer should be put on chart paper so that the list can remain posted as students read the section of the reading selection in which the words first appear. Introduce words in subsequent Discussion Guides similarly.

Vocabulary List A

meticulously (p. 3)	disdainfully (p. 11)	dubious (p. 21)
disposition (p. 4)	amiably (p. 11)	*monotonously (p. 22)
*concession (p. 4)	sheepishly (p. 15)	*audible (p. 22)
intriguing (p. 4)	expansive (p. 15)	temerity (p. 23)
admonished (p. 4)	transposed (p. 15)	appalled (p. 23)
testily (p. 4)	sufficiently (p. 15)	furrowed (p. 24)
raucous (p. 5)	*emblem (p. 15)	*indignant (p. 24)
pensively (p. 6)	knell (p. 15)	diction (p. 29)
sharecropping (p. 6)	milling (p. 16)	*dismayed (p. 29)
mortgage (p. 6)	abounded (p. 17)	noncommittal (p. 29)
emaciated (p. 8)	reverberated (p. 18)	maverick (p. 30)
jauntily (p. 8)	extended (p. 18)	imperiously (p. 31)
undaunted (p. 8)	quizzically (p. 19)	
morosely (p. 11)	ebbed (p. 21)	

Special Glossary

Reconstruction - the United States government program of reorganizing and rebuilding the South after the American Civil War

Yankees - people from the North

Glossary of Starred Words

concession - a compromise

emblem - a symbol or sign

monotonously - in a boring, tiresome, repetitive way

audible - able to be heard

indignant - offended; resentful; "put out"

dismayed - disappointed; upset

Sample Meaningful Sentences for Starred Words

1. John didn't really want to help his sister with her homework, but his mother insisted, so he made a **concession** and said he would do it after he watched his favorite show.

2. The cheerleaders had the team **emblem**, a picture of a grinning alligator head, sewn on their sweatshirts so that everyone would know which team they supported.

3. When I saw how **monotonously** Mr. Tolliver read the lesson to the class, never once changing his expression, I understood why the students were bored.

4. Shakira turned up the volume on the radio so high that I was afraid it would be **audible** all over the block.

5. Damien always had the highest grades in his class in math, so he was shocked and **indignant** when he did not receive the Math Prize at the end of the school year.

6. I was **dismayed** when I realized that all my hard work preparing for my geography test was useless, because I had studied the wrong chapter.

 **The Writer's Craft**

Characterization

Characterization is the way an author develops characters so that readers can picture and understand them. There are several different ways we learn about a character. One is the author's description of the character. Another is the character's own words and actions. Finally, we can learn about a character by observing the way other characters in the book relate to him or her. Each of these things is like a piece of a puzzle. When we put them together, we should be able to get a good idea of a character's personality.

In chapter 1, the writer gives us a wonderful introduction to Cassie Logan and her three brothers, Stacey, Christopher-John, and Little Man, as well as their friends T.J. and Claude. As you read, notice how she reveals each child's character. How are they similar? How are they different?

DISCUSSION QUESTIONS AND ACTIVITIES

Section I. Read chapter 1 (pp. 3-31). Discuss your responses to the questions and activities with a classmate. Then write your answers separately.

1. **The Logan land is so important to the family that important sacrifices are made to keep it. What are some of these sacrifices? Can you explain why the land is so important to Papa?** One sacrifice that the Logans make to keep their land is that Papa goes away for months at a time to work on the railroad. In addition, Mama teaches school and runs the farm, Big Ma (Cassie's grandmother) works in the fields and keeps the house, and the children wear old, worn clothing so that there will be enough money to pay the mortgage and the taxes. The land is important to Papa because it represents the family's independence.

2. **Why don't Cassie, Christopher-John, or Little Man like T.J.? Why do you think Stacey does like him?** Cassie, Christopher-John, and Little Man dislike T.J. for several reasons. For one thing, he teases them by giving out information as slowly as possible. Secondly, he avoids being whipped for going to the Wallace store by lying to his mother and telling her that he went there to fetch Claude, which brings Claude a whipping he does not deserve. Finally, T.J. laughs at Little Man's dismay when the school bus sprays red dust all over his best clothes. He is also shifty and dishonest, trying to draw Stacey into his own schemes for cheating his way through the seventh grade. Stacey is aware of these qualities and disapproves of them. However, he tends to overlook T.J.'s bad qualities, probably because T.J. is the nearest neighbor around his own age, and he wants to maintain that friendship.

3. **Why don't Little Man and Cassie want their books? Do you agree with their position? Explain why or why not.** Little Man and Cassie do not want their books partly because the books are worn-out ones that the white schools no longer want, but mostly because a highly offensive racial slur is used to identify the books' recipients on the inside front cover. Answers may vary as to whether students agree with their position.

4. **Why do the other teachers consider Mama a "maverick"? How is her point of view different from Miss Crocker's?** The other teachers consider Mama a maverick because her ideas are too radical for them. Miss Crocker is willing to accept the books that the Board of Education has given the school. She does not want to complain about their poor condition or the racially offensive material on the inside cover because she doesn't want to get in trouble, and, apparently, because she has accepted the status quo of race relations as they exist. Mama, on the other hand, agrees with Cassie and Little Man that this is not acceptable. She is willing to risk the disapproval of the Board of Education by pasting paper over the offensive material, because she believes this is necessary to maintain her own dignity and that of her students.

5. **Think about the four Logan children introduced in this chapter (Cassie, Stacey, Christopher-John, and Little Man), T.J. Avery, and Jeremy Simms. Using the Character Portrait pages at the end of this Guide (pages 34-39 in Student's Guide), list at least one character trait for each child. Then, show evidence for this character trait from his or her actions, thoughts, or words. (Please note: You do not have to fill in all of the boxes at this time. You will have an opportunity to fill in more character traits as the book goes on.)** Some possible answers for this question are shown (other answers are also possible; see "Guided Discussion," page 12).

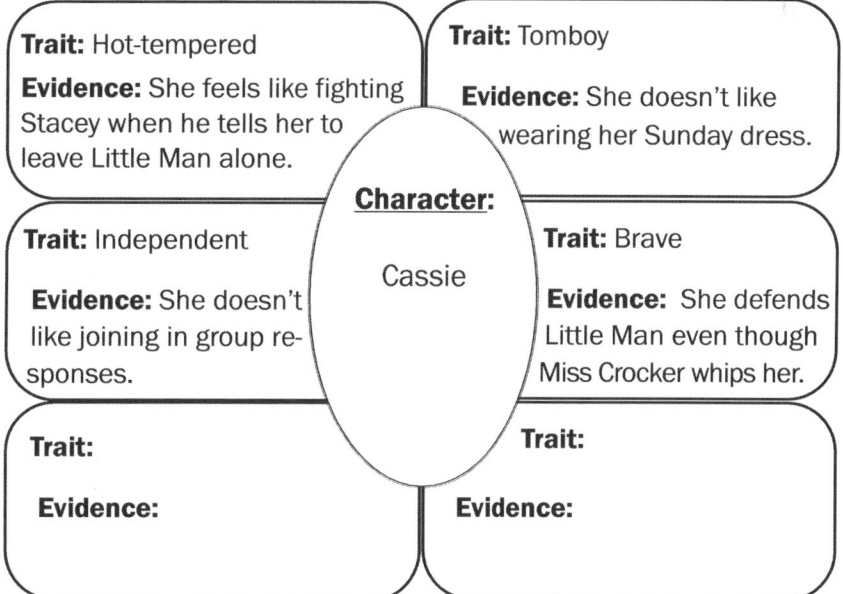

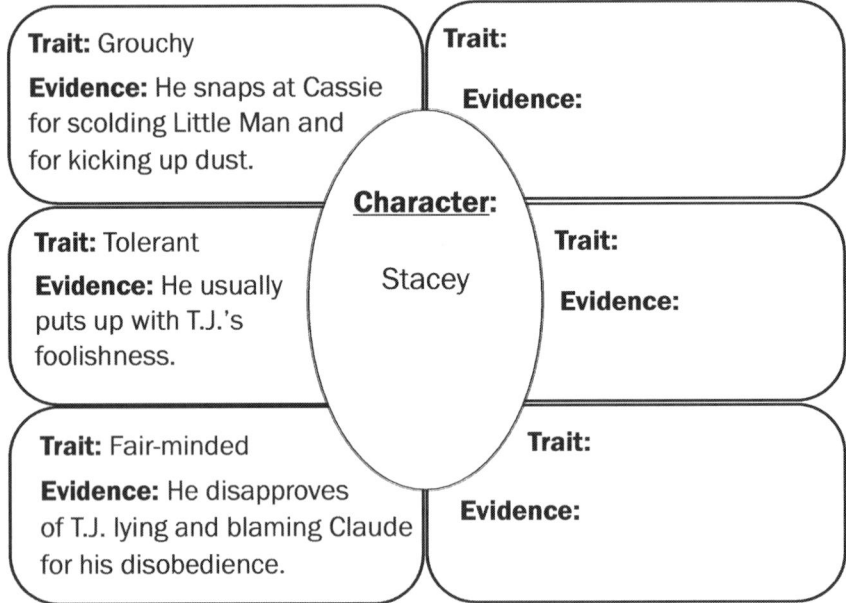

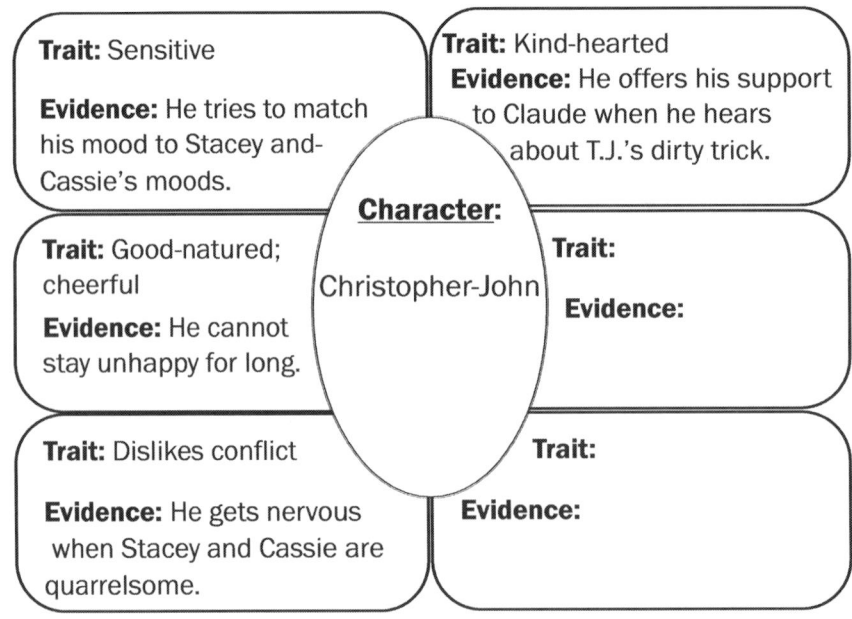

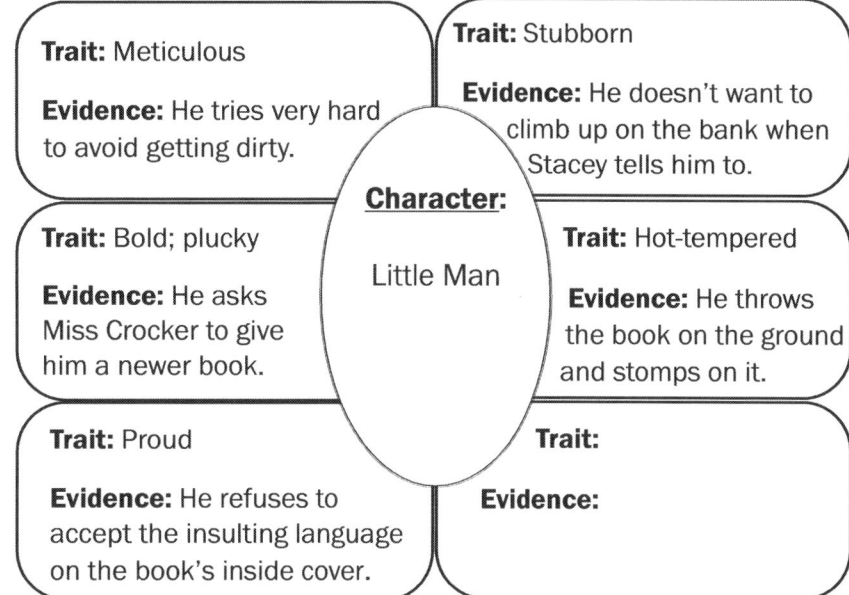

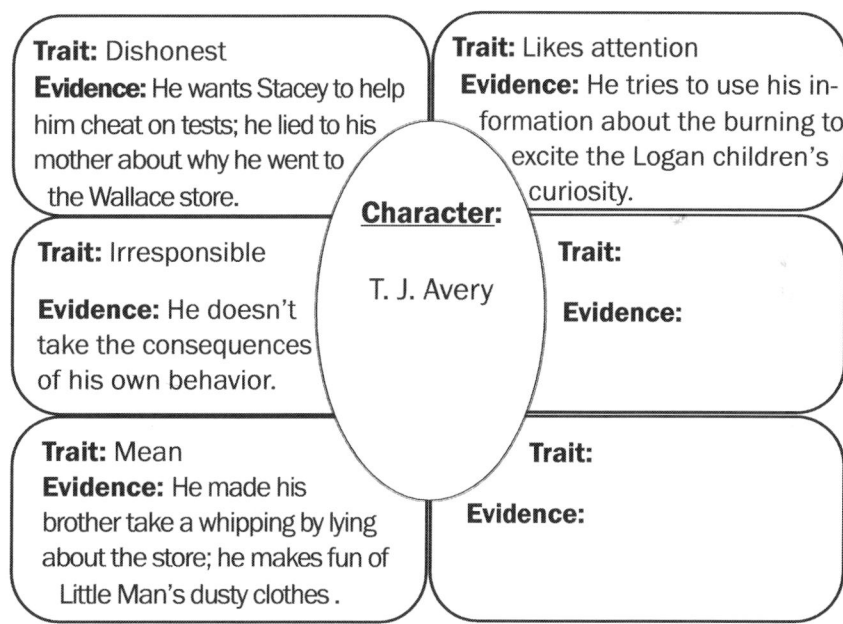

TEACHER'S MANUAL
Chapters 1–3

Trait: Friendly
Evidence: He walks part way to and from school with the Logan children every day.

Trait: Patient/ persevering
Evidence: He continues to be friendly with the Logans even though they don't encourage him very much.

Character: Jeremy Simms

Trait: Lonely
Evidence: He doesn't seem to have many white friends.

Trait:
Evidence:

Trait: Courageous
Evidence: He spends time with black people even though white people mock him and sometimes beat him for it.

Trait: Thinks for himself
Evidence: He enjoys the Logans' company more than many people he knows. He senses how unfair racial prejudice is.

Make A Prediction:

What do you think Mama and Cassie will talk about?

Guided Discussion:

Discuss some of the key questions and activities in Section I. In addition, feel free to include in your discussion questions that are not in the Discussion Guide. For example, *What does Jeremy do that is unusual? Why do you think he does this? What does this suggest about the kind of person Jeremy is?* Jeremy walks part of the way to school with the Logans every day, although he is white and most white people don't want to have anything to do with African Americans. Answers may vary as to why he does this. He may simply be lonely; he may also find the Logans more attractive as friends than the white people around him, and he may be taking a stand against racism in his own quiet way.

In a similar way, go over the "Character Portrait" graphic organizers for each of the six characters. **A black line master** for making transparencies for the Character Portraits is provided at the end of this TEACHER'S MANUAL (page 63). As a class, working with the transparencies, begin to fill out each of the character portraits. Make sure students realize that they should not fill up all of the space on their graphic organizers, because they will continue to add to them after reading subsequent chapters. In fact, it would be wise to leave one or more boxes empty for each character in case new traits are observed later on.

✔ Prediction Check-up

Return to the vocabulary prediction chart, and use it to check the predictions students made prior to reading this section of the reading selection. Remind students that, even if their predictions did not prove true, the value was in making them.

Vocabulary List B

scoffed (p. 32)	coddling (p. 45)	recklessly (p. 53)
formidable (p. 34)	penetrate (p. 46)	careen (p. 54)
chiffonier (p. 36)	flippantly (p. 47)	disgruntled (p. 56)
resiliency (p. 42)	glowered (p. 48)	gloat (p. 57)
attired (p. 43)	*relent (p. 49)	haggard (p. 63)
*endured (p. 43)	conspiratorially (p. 50)	listlessly (p. 63)
*inaccessible (p. 43)	stealthily (p. 50)	adamantly (p. 64)
emitted (p. 43)	*oblivious (p. 51)	transfixed (p. 66)
dejected (p. 44)	intensity (p. 53)	precariously (p. 66)

Glossary of Starred Words

endured - put up with; bore

inaccessible - impossible to get to or reach

relent - to give in

oblivious - not aware of; not bothered by

Sample Meaningful Sentences for Starred Words

1. Juanita **endured** her sister's cruel teasing every time she got a bad grade, but she found it very painful.

2. Mother put the dangerous cleaning products on the highest shelf of a locked cupboard so they would be **inaccessible** to the young children in the house.

3. Teyonna was not usually allowed to go to boy-girl parties, but she begged her mother to **relent** just this once so she could attend her cousin's birthday celebration.

4. Absorbed in his mystery novel, Brandon was so **oblivious** to the noises around him that he didn't even realize the lunch bell had rung.

 **The Writer's Craft**

First Person Point of View

Most often, stories are told by narrators who are outside the action of the story. They may or may not have insight into the thoughts and feelings of the characters, whom they refer to using pronouns such as "he," "she," and "they." This is called the **third person point of view**.

However, sometimes writers choose to tell the story from the point of view of one of the characters in the story, as if it were the character himself or herself writing. The writer uses pronouns like "I," "me," "we," and "our." The words and ideas used in the storytelling are words and ideas that the character would use. This is called the **first person point of view**.

Roll of Thunder, Hear My Cry is told from the first person point of view. As you read, notice how hearing the story from Cassie's point of view affects what we know – and what we don't know – about what is going on.

DISCUSSION QUESTIONS AND ACTIVITIES

Section II. Read chapters 2 and 3 (pages 32-68). Discuss your responses to the questions and activities with a classmate. Then write your answers separately.

1. **Why do you think Cassie says Papa brought Mr. Morrison home because of the burning at the Berry farm? Why doesn't Papa want the children to go to the Wallaces' store?**
Cassie says Papa brought Mr. Morrison home because of the burning since she believes that Papa is concerned for the family's safety while he is away. Mr. Morrison is a very powerful man, and Cassie imagines that Papa has asked him to protect the family as well as help out with the farm work.

Papa doesn't want the children to go to the Wallaces' store because he expects that one day there will be a lot of trouble for young people who hang around the store. He expects trouble because he has heard that the young people drink liquor at the store, and also because he believes that the Wallaces want to make trouble for the African-American young people.

2. **How is the Great Faith Elementary and Secondary School different from the Jefferson Davis School? (Hint: reviewing chapter 1 will help you answer this question.) What are some ways that both of these schools are different from your school?** The most obvious difference between Great Faith and the Jefferson Davis School is that Great Faith is a school for African Americans, while only white children are allowed to attend Jefferson Davis. For this reason, Jefferson Davis receives a much greater share of county resources and, therefore, is better equipped. Jefferson Davis students ride in school buses and use recent textbooks in good condition. By contrast, Great Faith is supported mainly by the church. Its students walk to school, and they receive only worn, outdated textbooks that are no longer wanted. The buildings at Great Faith are old and worn and there are no sports fields. At Great Faith, school lasts only six months, because the children are needed in the cotton fields from April through September, whereas the Jefferson Davis school year begins in August and probably also ends later in the spring.

   Answers will vary as to how these schools differ from your students' school. In any case, however, it is worth noting that today children of all races are allowed to attend the same schools. (Some students may point out that de facto segregation is still a reality in many places; this is a valid point and could give rise to an interesting class discussion.)

3. **Why does Cassie describe the bus as "a living thing, plaguing and defeating us at every turn" (p. 46)?** Cassie describes the bus in this way because the bus driver and the white children take pleasure in spraying the African-American children with mud. The driver speeds up or swerves when necessary to make sure that he gets the children dirty. Even when they leave the house early, it seems that the bus often manages to splash them anyway.

4. **How do the children treat Jeremy after the bus gets them dirty? Do you think this is fair? Why or why not?** After the bus gets them dirty, the children are rude and unfriendly to Jeremy,

even though he tries to be friendly to them. Answers may vary as to whether students think this is fair. While the children's frustration and pent-up fury is certainly understandable, it can hardly be called fair. Jeremy is obviously not responsible for the cruelty of the bus driver and his passengers, and in fact, Cassie suddenly realizes that Jeremy consistently refrains from riding the bus, despite the rain and chill.

5. **How do the children feel when they hear that the white men are going to make trouble again? Why do they react this way?** The children are very frightened when they hear that the white men are going to make trouble again, because they are afraid it is their fault. They dug a ditch in the road where the bus had splashed them, and the bus got bogged down and broke an axle. The children are afraid the white men are after them. The younger boys wonder whether they will be set afire as the Berrys were. Stacey feels especially upset because he feels guilty for involving the other children in such a rash venture

Make A Prediction:

Will the men come back to hurt the Logans?

Guided Discussion:

Discuss some of the key questions and activities in Section II. In addition, feel free to include in your discussion questions that are not in the Discussion Guide. Ask students whether they have anything to add to their Character Portraits. They may wish to add "determined" or "a leader" to Stacey's qualities, based on his initiative in organizing the children to sabotage the school bus, and also "responsible" or "conscientious," because of his feelings of guilt when he realizes his actions may have brought great danger on them.

 ### Prediction Check-up

Return to the vocabulary prediction chart, and use it to check the predictions students made prior to reading this section of the reading selection. Remind students that, even if their predictions did not prove true, the value was in making them.

Selection Review

1. **List some of the reasons that Cassie, Christopher-John, and Little Man dislike T.J.** The children dislike T.J. because he is dishonest. He wants Stacey to help him cheat at school. He is also mean. Instead of taking his punishment, he lies so that his mother will punish his little brother Claude instead. He laughs at Little Man when his clothes get dirty. T.J. also makes the children angry by teasing them with tidbits of gossip.

2. **Why do Cassie and Little Man get in trouble the first day of school? How does Mama show that she agrees with them?** Cassie and Little Man get in trouble on the first day of school because they do not want their "new" school textbooks. Little Man does not want his book at first because it is old, dirty, and in poor condition. When he takes the book anyway, he finds insulting words about the students' race written on the inside cover. He throws the book on the floor and jumps on it. When Cassie tries to explain to Miss Crocker why Little Man is angry, Miss Crocker becomes angry with both children. However, when Miss Crocker reports their behavior to Mama, Mama pastes paper over the inside cover. Cassie realizes that Mama understands why the children were angry.

3. **Why is Papa concerned about the family's safety? What does he do to try to protect them?** Papa is concerned about the family's safety because some white men set fire to three African Americans, killing one of them. Papa takes two safety measures to protect the family. He asks his friend, Mr. Morrison, to stay with them while he is away working for the railroad. Mr. Morrison is a huge, powerful man. Papa hopes that he will be able to keep danger away. Papa also strictly warns the children to stay away from the Wallaces' store. He is afraid that some day there will be serious trouble for the young people who spend time there.

4. **Describe two ways the children express their anger after the bus soaks them with mud. Which reaction do you think was fairer?** After the bus splashes them, the children express their anger by being unfriendly to Jeremy. They also express their anger by digging a big ditch in the road. The Jefferson Davis bus breaks down and the white children have to walk home. Although this causes a lot of trouble, in a way it is fairer, because it punishes the people who caused the problem. The bus driver

and the white children who laughed find out how it feels to walk home soaked with mud. They also have to walk to school every day for several weeks. On the other hand, being unfriendly to Jeremy is not fair. In their anger, the children are hurting someone who tries to be nice to them. Jeremy had nothing to do with the problem. He never even rides the bus.

5. Why do the children feel frightened and guilty when they hear that the white men are going to make trouble again?
The children are frightened when they hear that the white men plan to make trouble because they think that the men are angry with them for making the bus break down. They are especially frightened because they know that white men set the Berry men on fire. They wonder whether they will be burned up too. The children, especially Stacey, feel guilty because they think they have brought more trouble to their community.

Literature-Related Writing

1. Imagine that one of the Logan children (Cassie, Stacey, Christopher-John or Little Man) were to take a ride in a time machine and visit your school today. What would seem surprising to him or her? Write a **short story** of four or five paragraphs describing the child's reaction to the way things are in schools today.

2. The writer of *Roll of Thunder, Hear My Cry* uses action and dialogue, as well as description, to make the characters in her story seem real to us. Write a **short story** about yourself and two or three of your siblings, cousins, or close friends. The situations and events can be fictional (made up), but try to use real people you know as characters in the story. Try to show the different personalities of the characters through their words (the dialogue) and their actions.

3. Think back to when you were in elementary school. Write a narrative account from the **first person point of view** describing something that happened to you in elementary school that had an important impact on your life.

 **Extension Activities**

1. Make a model of Great Faith Elementary and Secondary School, based on the description given in chapter 1.
2. With other students, act out the incident in which Little Man and Cassie tell Miss Crocker that they do not want their "new" books.
3. Draw or paint an illustration for a scene from the book.

Literature Test

1. **Tell why you think T.J. would not be a very good friend, giving examples from the story.** Students should mention several of the following reasons: T.J. would not be a good friend because he tries to drag his friends into trouble with him; for example, he suggests that Stacey could help him cheat in school. He is also dishonest, and does not hesitate to lie so that someone else – his brother Claude – takes the punishment he should have received. He has a mean streak, and laughs at Little Man when he is upset. He likes to tease his friends with gossip so that he can be the center of attention. Also, he talks too much and does not know how to keep a secret.

2. **Explain why Cassie and Little Man refuse to take their "new" textbooks. How does Mama's reaction to their "misbehavior" differ from Miss Crocker's?** Cassie and Little Man's "new" textbooks are actually old and worn. However, the real reason the children refuse to take them is that racial slurs are written on the inside cover. Miss Crocker whips them for being disobedient, but Mama understands why they are angry. She pastes paper over the offensive writing on the inside cover.

3. **Why does Papa bring Mr. Morrison to stay with the family? Why does he warn the children to stay away from the Wallaces' store?** Papa brings Mr. Morrison home mainly to protect the family from white men who might try to hurt them. He tells the children to stay away from the Wallaces' store because he does not like the Wallaces, and he is afraid that there will be serious trouble for the young people who hang out there.

4. **The evening after they dig a ditch to make the white children's school bus break down, the Logan children are so excited and proud that they cannot stop giggling. What happens to make their feelings change to fear and guilt?** The children's feelings change to fear and guilt when they hear that the white men are riding around again looking for trouble. They are afraid the men are looking for them, and they feel guilty because they believe their actions have brought trouble down on the whole African-American community.

Discussion Guide #2

Chapters 4-6 (pages 69-139)

Vocabulary List A

churn (v., p. 69)	prolong (p. 74)	*engrossed (p. 85)
absurd (p. 71)	ploy (p. 74)	*subtle (p. 88)
expounding (p. 72)	mercantile (p. 75)	ransacked (p. 91)
discourse (n., p. 72)	authoritatively (p. 75)	emphatic (p. 93)
haughtily (p. 73)	retrieve (p. 75)	fathom (v., p. 96)
*prevailed (p. 73)	chided (p. 77)	warily (p. 96)
riveted (p. 73)	aloof (p. 77)	*patronize (p. 98)
feigned (p. 74)	*discreetly (p. 78)	disfigured (adj., p. 98)

Glossary of Starred Words

prevailed - was widespread or was stronger

discreetly - tactfully; without calling attention to oneself

engrossed - very interested in; absorbed

subtle - not obvious

patronize - to shop at

Sample Meaningful Sentences for Starred Words

1. The children crowded noisily into the recreation center, but their interest in the puppet theater overcame their rowdiness and soon a hushed silence **prevailed** in the room.

2. Felicia went out of the room to blow her nose **discreetly** where no one could hear her.

3. The movie was very exciting, and we soon became so **engrossed** in watching it that we did not even notice that Mom had brought us a bowl of popcorn.

4. Candace felt it would be rude to tell her friend bluntly that she was not interested in spreading gossip, so she tried to give her a **subtle** hint by changing the subject instead.

5. The community association encouraged us to **patronize** local stores for our Christmas shopping, rather than making our purchases at the big suburban malls.

The Writer's Craft

Dialect

Dialect is a regional variance in language that may include differences in grammar, vocabulary, and pronunciation. In *Roll of Thunder, Hear My Cry,* some of the characters use dialect while others do not. Can you explain this? How does the use of dialect make the characters seem more realistic?

DISCUSSION QUESTIONS AND ACTIVITIES

Section I. Read chapter 4 (pages 69-101). Discuss your responses to the questions and activities with a classmate. Then write your answers separately.

1. **In the boxes of the sequence chain below, list the circumstances that lead Stacey to disobey Papa's order to stay away from the Wallaces' store. Do you think it is right or wrong for Stacey to do this? Why?** Some possible answers for the sequence chain are shown.

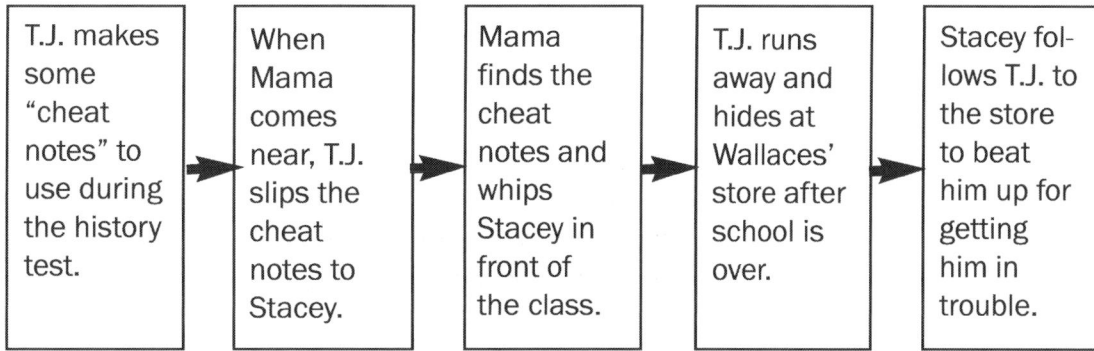

Answers may vary as to whether Stacey's actions are right or wrong. The main positions may be summarized as follows:

(1) Some students, and probably most adults, may say that Stacey should have told Mama the truth when asked where the cheat notes came from. It is impossible for a person in authority to act fairly without accurate information. By telling the truth, Stacey would enable Mama to discipline T.J. justly. Stacey would not need to "take the law into his own hands," as it were, by fighting with T.J. after school.

(2) Many students, and some adults, may feel that Stacey did the right thing in refusing to "tell on" T.J. Most adults would probably say that in taking this position, Stacey assumes responsibility for the situation. This does not necessarily mean he has to beat T.J. up after school – at the Wallaces' store or anywhere else. He could have applied pressure on T.J. to turn himself in, for example, by withdrawing his friendship.

(3) Even if we accept the dubious premise that Stacey should "teach T.J. a lesson" by beating him up, Stacey does not have to follow T.J. to the Wallaces' store to do so. T.J. would have come home eventually.

It seems clear that Stacey was not really justified in disobeying his parents by going to the store. He had a number of other options and, in his anger, just did not consider them.

2. **Why does Mr. Morrison let Stacey decide whether to tell Mama about going to the store? How does this change Stacey's feelings toward Mr. Morrison?** When he stops the fight, Mr. Morrison lets Stacey decide whether to tell Mama because he wants Stacey to take responsibility for his own actions. He explains to the children why their parents do not allow them to go to the store and leaves the decision up to Stacey. This makes Stacey begin to like and appreciate Mr. Morrison. Before, he resented him because he thought that Mr. Morrison's presence implied that Papa did not trust Stacey to take care of the family in his absence. The way Mr. Morrison handles this situation makes Stacey feel that Mr. Morrison respects him and is treating him like a man.

3. **Why do you think Mr. Jamison had sold 200 acres to Paul Edward Logan, Cassie's grandfather, rather than to Mr. Granger? Why doesn't Big Ma want to sell the farm to Mr.**

Granger? Answers may vary as to why Mr. Jamison sold the land to Paul Logan rather than to Mr. Granger. However, Mr. Jamison probably admired Paul Logan's far-sightedness, hard work, and initiative, both in paying off and keeping the first 200 acres, and in wanting to buy 200 more. Also, Mr. Jamison is a fair-minded man. He knew that Mr. Granger had more land than he needed already. Mr. Jamison probably wanted to offer the Logans the opportunity to make better use of the additional 200 acres than Mr. Granger was likely to. Big Ma is determined not to sell the land to Mr. Granger because she and her husband invested years of backbreaking work in it. It carries precious memories for her and is Paul Edward's legacy to her and to her two remaining sons, Uncle Hammer and Papa.

4. **Why does Mama take the children to see Mr. Berry? Why does she try to convince people in the African-American community to stop shopping at the Wallaces' store?** Mama takes the children to see Mr. Berry so they will understand what a terrible thing the Wallaces did to him, and why she does not want them to have anything to do with the Wallaces. She tries to convince people to stop shopping at the store because the Wallaces have a bad influence in the community. They take the people's money and encourage the young people to smoke and drink.

5. **Turn to the "Character Portrait" pages for Stacey and T.J. Add any new character traits and/or supporting evidence for these two characters found in this chapter.** Some possible additions might be:

Stacey – Honest: He refuses to cheat and tries to prevent T.J. from doing so.

Sense of honor: He refuses to get other people in trouble.

Responsible or Brave: He admits to Mama that he went to Wallaces' store.

T.J. – [Dishonest]: He makes a cheat sheet for the history test, then slips his notes to Stacey so he won't get in trouble.

[Irresponsible]: He lets Stacey take the whipping that he (T.J.) deserved.

Make A Prediction:

Who will be able to back people's credit so they can shop in Vicksburg?

Guided Discussion:

Discuss some of the key questions and activities in Section I. In addition, feel free to include in your discussion questions that are not in the Discussion Guide. For example, you might ask, *How do the children feel when they find out that the white men were angry with Mr. Tatum? Why do they feel this way?* The children feel relieved when they learn that the white men's anger was directed at Mr. Tatum. They feel this way because it means that their role in making the bus break down has not been suspected. It is not their fault that the white men's anger has been aroused, and they can stop being afraid of some terrible reckoning catching up with them.

Also, make sure that students understand the issues and risks involved for the sharecropping families in Mama's plan to boycott the Wallaces' store. Point out that the sharecroppers' dependence on the plantation owners is one reason why the Logans are so fiercely determined to hold on to their own land.

Make sure you address the questions found in the Writer's Craft Box on **dialect**. Some characters speak in dialect and others do not because of their differing educational backgrounds and concerns. Mama, in particular, never uses dialect because she has been trained as a teacher, and education is important to her. However, the everyday speech of most of the other characters, who have not received a college education, is Southern dialect. This is especially noticeable in Big Ma's long discussion with Cassie about the farm. The characters' use of dialogue is realistic and makes us feel that the account is authentic.

Prediction Check-up

Return to the vocabulary prediction chart, and use it to check the predictions students made prior to reading this section of the reading selection. Remind students that, even if their predictions did not prove true, the value was in making them.

Vocabulary List B

*subdued (adj., p. 103)
wheedle (p. 104)
envisioned (p. 104)
spindly (p. 104)
gingerly (p. 106)
promenading (p. 107)
reluctantly (p. 109)
bland (p. 110)
recoiled (p. 111)
emerged (p. 112)
*retaliated (p. 112)
malevolently (p. 112)
ambled (p. 113)
balked (p. 116)
dumbfounded (p. 119)
nattily (p. 119)
mutely (p. 121)
confounded (adj., p. 122)
muffle (p. 122)
*ominously (p. 124)
reprimand (n., p. 125)
profitable (p. 128)
vanity (p. 132)
*resigned (adj., p. 133)
reverently (p. 135)
snidely (p. 136)

Glossary of Starred Words

subdued - quiet; restrained

retaliated - shot back; paid back "tit for tat"

ominously - threateningly

resigned - accepting of something but not happy about it

Sample Meaningful Sentences for Starred Words

1. Dad said I could not go outside to play until I fulfilled my **obligations** to clean my room and finish my homework.

2. Every time Christopher poked his little sister with his elbow, she **retaliated** by kicking him right back.

3. "If your report card does not improve this term," Dad declared **ominously**, "you will not be allowed to participate in any sports or extracurricular activities."

4. "I would rather go out with my friends, but since my mother has to work, I guess I have to stay with my little sister again, " Marissa said with a **resigned** sigh.

 **The Writer's Craft**

Setting

Setting is a term used to describe the time and place in which the action of a story occurs. The setting of *Roll of Thunder, Hear My Cry* is Mississippi in the 1930s. More specifically, most of the action up to this point has taken place within the African-American community of Spokane County. In chapter 5, the story takes us farther away from Cassie's home for the first time, to the nearby town of Strawberry. What do you notice about Strawberry: the sights, the sounds, the people? How does Cassie's first visit to Strawberry change her view of life? How do you think it might affect her feelings about the family farm?

DISCUSSION QUESTIONS AND ACTIVITIES

Section II. Read chapters 5 and 6 (pages 102-139). Discuss your responses to the questions and activities with a classmate. Then write your answers separately.

1. **List the things that surprise and anger Cassie on her first visit to Strawberry. What does Cassie's indignation tell us about the way she has been raised?** Cassie is surprised that Big Ma parks her wagon in the back of the field to sell her butter and eggs. She has to do this because the space at the front of the field is for white people. Cassie is also angry because Mr. Barnett begins to fill T.J.'s order, then stops to serve a number of white people, including a young girl. When Cassie tries to

remind Mr. Barnett that they have been waiting a long time, Mr. Barnett becomes very angry and shouts at her, then makes the children leave the store. Finally, when Cassie accidentally bumps into Lillian Jean Simms, Lillian Jean insists that she not only apologize, but also step down off the sidewalk and walk in the dust. When Cassie resists, Mr. Simms grabs her arm and knocks her off the sidewalk. He also makes her apologize again, calling Lillian Jean "Miz Lillian Jean." Cassie's indignation shows that her parents have raised her to believe that people are equal and deserving of equal treatment and respect, whatever their race. She has not been taught to accept racial discrimination as the "normal" thing, although most people do consider it normal in Mississippi in the 1930s.

2. **Why does Cassie like Mr. Jamison?** Cassie likes Mr. Jamison because he is respectful to her family. He addresses Mama and Big Ma as "Missus," unlike other white people Cassie knows. She also likes him because he gives straightforward answers to questions.

3. **Do you think it is right or wrong for Cassie to be angry with Mr. Barnett and Lillian Jean? Why do you think Big Ma makes Cassie apologize to Lillian Jean?** Most students will probably agree that Cassie has every right to be upset with Mr. Barnett, as well as with Lillian Jean, since both Mr. Barnett and Lillian Jean obviously acted unfairly. Big Ma herself is undoubtedly angry about the situation, but she does not see any other choice but to make Cassie apologize. She is afraid that Mr. Simms will hurt Cassie or that the incident might provoke violence from the large crowd that has gathered around them.

4. **How is Uncle Hammer different from most of the African Americans living in Mississippi? Which way of dealing with racism do you think would be more effective: Uncle Hammer's way or Mama's way?** Uncle Hammer is different from most African Americans living in Mississippi in that he refuses to repress his anger over racial injustice. He is not afraid of what the white people will do to him if he meets violence with violence. Until Mr. Morrison manages to dissuade him, he fully intends to go to the Simms' house and punish Mr. Simms for knocking Cassie down. Uncle Hammer's way of fighting back is violent and reckless. It does not give people an opportunity to change. If Uncle Hammer really hurt a white person or burned something down, he would probably be killed. This would be

bad for the entire family and the community. Mama's way, getting the community to work together, is slower, but it has a better chance of having some effect.

5. **Begin to fill out the Character Portrait (page 40 in Student's Guide) for Uncle Hammer. Also, consider whether you might want to add traits and/or supporting evidence to your Character Portraits of the Logan children.** Some possible answers for Uncle Hammer's Character Portrait might be:

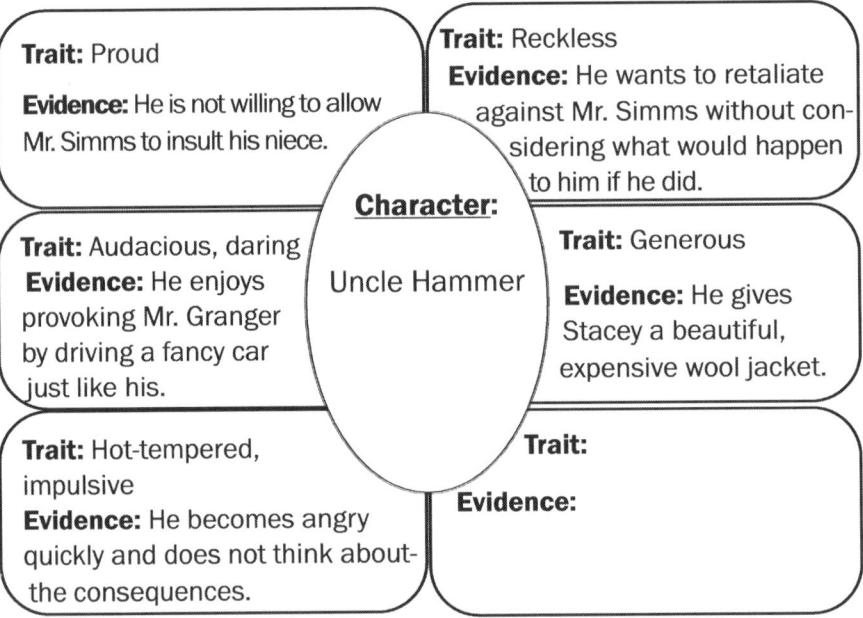

Trait: Proud
Evidence: He is not willing to allow Mr. Simms to insult his niece.

Trait: Reckless
Evidence: He wants to retaliate against Mr. Simms without considering what would happen to him if he did.

Character: Uncle Hammer

Trait: Audacious, daring
Evidence: He enjoys provoking Mr. Granger by driving a fancy car just like his.

Trait: Generous
Evidence: He gives Stacey a beautiful, expensive wool jacket.

Trait: Hot-tempered, impulsive
Evidence: He becomes angry quickly and does not think about the consequences.

Trait:
Evidence:

Some possible additions to the children's Character Portraits might be:

Stacey – [Responsible]: He tries to keep Cassie out of trouble.

[Fair-minded]: He tries to help Cassie understand why Big Ma acted as she did.

Cassie – [Hot-tempered]: She shouts at Mr. Barnett when he insults her.

Stubborn: She refuses to back down, even when Stacey tries to warn her.

Proud: She is hurt and indignant at the treatment she receives from Mr. Barnett and the Simms.

Christopher-John – [Sensitive or kind-hearted]: He sympathizes with Cassie's frustration.

Make A Prediction:

Will the Logans have to pay for Uncle Hammer's bold behavior? What do you think will happen?

Guided Discussion:

Discuss some of the key questions and activities in Section II. In addition, feel free to include in your discussion questions that are not in the Discussion Guide. Be sure to discuss the issues raised in the Writer's Craft Box on **setting**. Cassie is disappointed by her first encounter with Strawberry; it is dirty and tired-looking. Most of the people seem to be farmers and their wives, in faded overalls and flour-sack dresses. More importantly, it is in Strawberry that Cassie encounters racism in a forceful way. She is appalled to realize that she and her family seem to have no rights that white people are bound to respect, not even those of common human decency. As Mama later explains to Cassie, poor, tired white farmers like Mr. Simms who have "little else to hold on to" cling all the more desperately to their illusion of racial superiority. We begin to realize that Cassie's parents have managed to shelter her from much of the force of racial discrimination at home. While the Logan family farm also suffers the effects of racial injustice, it has been an oasis of pride and dignity for the Logan children. Cassie's first encounter with the "outside world" comes as a very unpleasant shock to her.

 Prediction Check-up

Return to the vocabulary prediction chart, and use it to check the predictions students made prior to reading this section of the reading selection. Remind students that, even if their predictions did not prove true, the value was in making them.

Selection Review

1. **What are some ways Stacey could have solved his problem with T.J. *without* going to the Wallaces' store?** There are several ways that Stacey could have handled this situation differently. He could have told Mama the truth about where he got the answers for the history test. He could have taken T.J.'s punishment, but later told T.J. that they could not be friends unless T.J. told Mama the truth. Stacey could also have waited to deal with T.J. when he came home from the store.

2. **Why is Cassie's grandmother determined not to sell the family farm to Mr. Granger?** A Yankee bought a big piece of the Granger plantation after the Civil War. Cassie's grandfather, Paul Edward Logan, bought the first 200 acres from him. He paid off the mortgage and tried to buy more land. The younger Mr. Jamison finally sold him another 200 acres. Big Ma refuses to sell the land because she and her husband worked very hard to get it and keep it. It holds precious memories for her. It is the heritage Paul Edward left for her and her two living sons, Papa and Uncle Hammer.

3. **How does Mama make the children understand that the Wallaces are bad people? What does she want the African-American families to do to fight against the Wallaces' bad influence?** Mama takes the children to visit Mr. Berry. He is one of the men that the Wallaces set on fire. He is suffering terribly and hardly even looks like a human being. Mama wants the African-American families to keep their children away from the Wallaces' store. She also asks them to stop shopping there. She offers to help them get credit to shop in Vicksburg.

4. **Why does Cassie have a terrible day when she goes to Strawberry with Big Ma?** Cassie finds out in Strawberry how unfairly some white people treat African Americans. She is upset that Big Ma has to park her wagon at the back of the field. She becomes angry with Mr. Barnett, the storekeeper. He keeps her, Stacey, and T.J. waiting for a long time while he fills orders for white people. Finally, when Cassie bumps into Lillian Jean by accident, she has to apologize to her. Lillian Jean's father grabs Cassie's arm and knocks her down off the sidewalk. He forces Big Ma to make Cassie apologize again, calling Lillian Jean "Miz Lillian Jean."

5. **Mama and Uncle Hammer have different ways of fighting back against racism. Explain how their ways are different. Which way do you think is better?** Mama wants to fight against racism by getting the African-American community to work together. She wants them to show their feelings about bad treatment by not shopping at the Wallaces' store. Her way is non-violent. Uncle Hammer's way of fighting back is violent. He is ready to act alone. He does not think about the consequences. Uncle Hammer's way is dangerous. It does not give people an opportunity to change. If Uncle Hammer really hurt a white person or burned something down, he would probably be killed. This would be bad for the entire family and the community. Mama's way is slower, but it has a better chance of having some effect.

 ## Literature-Related Writing

1. Pretend you are Stacey. Write a **journal entry** about the day T.J. got you in trouble at school and you went to fight with him at the Wallaces' store. How did you feel about this situation after it was all over? What had you learned? What do you think of the part Mr. Morrison played?

2. Cassie had a terrible day in Strawberry because she found out how unfair life was. Did you ever have an experience that made you realize that life can be very unfair? Write a **personal narrative** telling what happened to you and how you reacted to this situation.

3. What do you think Mr. Morrison and Uncle Hammer talked about during the night? Write a **dialogue** between Mr. Morrison and Uncle Hammer, in which Mr. Morrison tries to convince Uncle Hammer that taking revenge on Mr. Simms is not a good idea.

 **Extension Activities**

1. Stacey got in trouble because T.J. was cheating in school. Conduct a survey OR organize a panel discussion in your class about cheating today. Attempt to answer the following questions: Why do students cheat? Why should you not cheat? What should you do if a friend cheats, or tries to involve you in cheating? What can students do to reduce the amount of cheating going on? What can teachers do?

2. With other students, act out the scene in which Cassie bumps into Lillian Jean and is forced to get off the sidewalk, as well as apologize to her. You will need students to play the roles of Cassie, Stacey, Lillian Jean, Jeremy, Mr. Simms, and Big Ma.

3. With another student, make an audio recording of the dialogue you wrote for Mr. Morrison and Uncle Hammer (Literature-Related Writing Activity #3). Play the tape for your class.

Literature Test

1. **Explain why Stacey gets in trouble at school.** Stacey gets in trouble because T.J. made "cheat notes" for the history test. When he saw Mama coming, he slipped the notes to Stacey. Mama found Stacey with the cheat notes. Stacey refuses to tell her where the notes came from, so she whips him.

2. **Why does Mama consider the Wallaces bad people? How does she want the African-American community to fight back against them?** Mama considers the Wallaces bad people because they set three men on fire. They also laugh at the African-American farmers even as they take their money and corrupt their young people with liquor. Mama wants the African-American families to keep their young people away from the Wallaces' store and to take their shopping somewhere else.

3. **Cassie says of her day in Strawberry, "No day in all my life had ever been as cruel as this one." Why does she say this? What happened that day?** Cassie's day in Strawberry was the cruelest one she had ever known because she learned just how unfair life could be for African Americans. First Big Ma had to park her wagon in the back of the market field. Then Mr. Barnett, the shopkeeper, kept the children waiting for a long

time while he waited on other customers. When Cassie protested, he insulted her and made her leave the store. When she bumped into Lillian Jean Simms, she had to apologize. Lillian Jean's father knocked her off the sidewalk and told Big Ma to make her apologize again, calling Lillian Jean "Miz Lillian Jean."

4. **How does Uncle Hammer react to the news that Mr. Simms knocked Cassie down? Why do Mama, Big Ma, and Mr. Morrison try to keep Uncle Hammer from going to the Simms' house?** Uncle Hammer becomes very angry when he learns that Mr. Simms knocked Cassie down. He wants to go after Mr. Simms to punish him. Mama, Big Ma, and Mr. Morrison try to dissuade him from going to the Simms' house because they know that if Uncle Hammer hurts Mr. Simms, he could be killed.

Discussion Guide #3

Chapters 7 and 8 (pages 140-194)

Vocabulary List A

bewildered (p. 142)
*apprehensive (p. 143)
*interminable (p. 144)
flaunting (p. 144)
consoling (v., p. 144)
deflate (p. 144)
faltering (adj., p. 144)
*restrained (p. 145)
interjected (p. 146)

shantytown (p. 147)
avenging (adj., p. 150)
retorted (p. 151)
*lingered (p. 158)
aristocracy (p. 159)
placid (p. 160)
*acknowledged (p. 160)
affirmed (p. 161)

*candidly (p. 161)
eviction (p. 163)
*boycott (n., p. 164)
*denote (p. 164)
sullenly (p. 166)
protrude (p. 167)
insolently (p. 168)
*condone (p. 168)

Special Glossary

Shreveport - a city in Louisiana

Rebel - refers to the Southern army in the Civil War

sabers - sharp curved swords used by officers during the Civil War

caldron - a large, heavy kettle or cooking pot

Glossary of Starred Words

apprehensive - fearful; nervous

interminable - without any end; very long

restrained - held back

lingered - spent extra time over something

continued on page 37

> **Glossary of Starred Words** continued
>
> **acknowledged** - paid attention to; responded to
>
> **candidly** - frankly; honestly; truthfully
>
> **boycott** - a group's refusal to do business with someone
>
> **denote** - to mean; to indicate; to imply
>
> **condone** - to overlook or excuse a wrong

Sample Meaningful Sentences for Starred Words

1. On the day of the final exam, I was so **apprehensive** that my stomach felt like it was tied in knots, because I knew I might fail the course if I did not do well.

2. The roll call lasted so long that it seemed **interminable**, and I had to wiggle my toes to keep my feet from falling asleep.

3. Bernard was so angry that he wanted to fight Jeff right there on the field, but his teammates grabbed him and **restrained** him so the umpire would not throw him out.

4. Mother's eyes **lingered** lovingly on Charlotte as she climbed into the airplane, as if she could hardly bear to say goodbye to her.

5. Bettina waved her hand wildly in the air until Miss Fisher finally **acknowledged** her and allowed her to answer the question.

6. Most teachers did not like to tell the students what their political views were, but Mr. Brewster expressed his opinion very **candidly** on a number of issues.

7. When we heard about the burger stand's sexist treatment of employees, our class declared a **boycott**, calling on students to stop eating there until the situation improved.

8. The bold letters beside the program listing in the television guide, such as Y, PG, or M, **denote** the age group for which the program is considered appropriate.

9. Although the teacher understood why Angela became angry with Sheila, she could not **condone** her decision to slap her, so she gave both of them after-school detention.

 **The Writer's Craft**

Flashback

A **flashback** is a scene that describes an event that occurred before the time in which the main story is set. A flashback might be presented through a dream, a dialogue, or a character's recollection. For example, Big Ma's memories of how Paul Edward, her husband, first bought the Logan land, form a flashback. There is a flashback in this chapter as well. What is it? Which character presents it? How does it help us to better understand this character's point of view on the Logans' situation?

DISCUSSION QUESTIONS AND ACTIVITIES

Section I. Read chapter 7 (pages 140-170). Discuss your responses to the questions and activities with a classmater. Then write your answers separately.

1. **Why do you think Mr. Morrison tells his story about the night men on Christmas Eve? Explain why Mama is reluctant for the children to hear the story, while Papa says they should hear it. Who do you think is right?** Mr. Morrison probably tells his story on Christmas Eve because it occurred on Christmas many years before, and because he wants the Logans to understand why he supports them so strongly in their own fight against racial injustice. Mama is reluctant for the children to hear the story because it involves burning and slashing, and Mr. Morrison's parents and sisters are all killed. Mama thinks the children might be frightened. However, Papa says they should hear it because it is part of their history as African Americans. He thinks they should be aware of this long legacy of injustice. Answers may vary as to which parent is right.

2. **Why do you think Jeremy gives Stacey the flute? Do you think Jeremy would be a better friend than T.J.? Why or why not?** Jeremy probably gives Stacey the flute as an expression of his desire for friendship with Stacey. It is true that Jeremy's personal qualities would probably make him a better friend than T.J. Jeremy is generous, courageous, and loyal to his principles, whereas T.J. is selfish, cowardly, and dishonest. He attempts to use Stacey for his own ends, and he mocks Stacey after having taken advantage of him. Unfortunately, the fact that Jeremy is one of the Simms would make friendship with him a risky venture, for Stacey as well as for Jeremy himself.

3. **Why do you think Stacey and his family are not very friendly to Jeremy? Do you think this is fair? Why or why not?** The Logans are not very friendly to Jeremy because they are not used to the idea of genuine friendship between blacks and whites. They are naturally suspicious of Jeremy's motives, and even when Papa grants that Jeremy's friendship may be sincere, he is afraid of the risks that it entails. Answers may vary somewhat as to whether this is fair. Certainly based on the Logans' past and present experience, their wariness is understandable and perhaps even prudent. However, it is not really fair to Jeremy to assume that because he is white his friendship is not to be trusted. Jeremy has already shown his willingness to suffer ostracism and even beating in his quiet pursuit of Stacey's friendship, and Stacey is probably right in sensing that Jeremy is not one to turn against him or look down on him when the boys grow older.

4. **What does Mr. Jamison expect to happen if the Logans boycott the Wallaces' store? Why do you think he offers to back the credit of the thirty families that want to do their shopping in Vicksburg?** Mr. Jamison does not expect the boycott will be successful. He believes that Mr. Granger and most of the other white people in the community will support the Wallaces, and that they will be too powerful for the Logans to beat. Mr. Jamison also realizes that the families shopping on credit will probably not be able to pay off all their debts, so he is likely to lose money by backing them. He will also face the anger of most of the other white people. However, he offers to do it anyway, because he disapproves of the racial injustice that takes place in the

county. He believes that the Logans' attempt to fight back is a good cause, and he wants to be part of it, even if it does not succeed. He also does not want the Logans to put up their land as collateral, for fear that Mr. Granger would seize the opportunity to take the land away from them.

5. **Why does Mr. Granger come to visit the Logans? Use the T-chart below. On one side, list reasons why Mr. Granger is unfriendly to Uncle Hammer. On the other side, list Uncle Hammer's reasons for being rude to Mr. Granger.** Mr. Granger comes to visit the Logans essentially to threaten that if they continue the boycott, he will use it to take the farm from them. Some possible answers for the T-chart are shown.

Why Mr. Granger Is Unfriendly	Why Uncle Hammer Is Rude
He wants African Americans to "stay in their place."	He resents Mr. Granger's treating African Americans like children.
He resents Uncle Hammer's going away to Chicago where Mr. Granger has no power over him.	He resents the low wages Mr. Granger pays laborers on his farm.
He resents the Logans' organizing the African Americans to defend their rights.	He considers Mr. Granger's offer to "straighten out the colored people's problems" hypocritical and insincere.
He resents Uncle Hammer's buying a car that looks like his.	He resents Mr. Granger's condoning the burning of the Berrys.
He resents Uncle Hammer's attitude, which he considers insolent and inappropriate.	He resents Mr. Granger's attitude, which he considers patronizing and insulting.

Make A Prediction:

How do you think Mr. Granger will try to get the Logans' farm? Do you think he will succeed?

Guided Discussion:

Discuss some of the key questions and activities in Section I. In addition, feel free to include in your discussion questions that are not in the Discussion Guide. Be sure to discuss the question found in the Writer's Craft Box on **Flashbacks**. The main flashback in this section is Mr. Morrison's tale of the night men. This flashback helps us to understand who Mr. Morrison is. We understand his physical size and power, because we learn that he is from "breeded stock" (make sure your students have understood what this means). We also understand that the terrible incident that took the lives of his parents is one that he will not forget. It has given him a lifelong determination not to submit to racial injustice, but to combat it shrewdly and intelligently, not underestimating the risks and the powerful forces behind it.

You might also suggest that your students think about the similarities and dissimilarities between Mr. Jamison and Jeremy Simms. You might want to draw a Venn diagram like the one below. Ask your students to list some similarities and some differences between Mr. Jamison and Jeremy Simms. *What is unusual about both of them?* Some possible responses are shown.

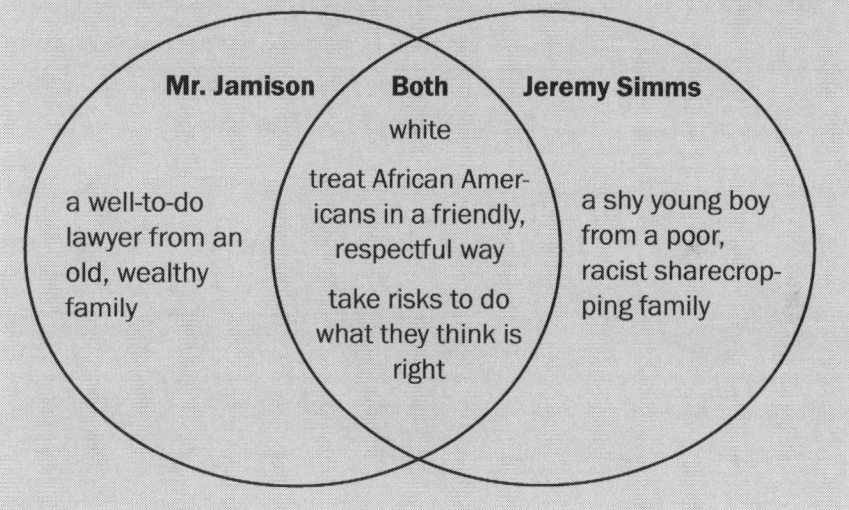

 **Prediction Check-up**

Return to the vocabulary prediction chart, and use it to check the predictions students made prior to reading this section of the reading selection. Remind students that, even if their predictions did not prove true, the value was in making them.

Vocabulary List B

piped (p. 172) apologetically (p. 179) *morosely (p. 188)
pondered (p. 176) glade (p. 180) fallow (p. 191)
confided (p. 177) banished (p. 182) shunned (p. 192)
jovial (p. 177) flinch (p. 183) testily (p. 192)
saunter (p. 179) reassurance (p. 186)

Starred Word Glossary

morosely - gloomily

Sample Meaningful Sentence

"There is no way at all that I could have passed that science test," Gregory sighed **morosely**, "because I left the whole second page completely blank."

The Writer's Craft

Foreshadowing

Foreshadowing is a word used to describe clues about events yet to occur in a story. We already know that T.J. is dishonest and irresponsible. There is no sign that he is learning from his mistakes. In chapter 8, there is yet another clue that T.J. is headed for serious trouble. As you read, try to spot this clue. What do you think will happen to T.J.?

DISCUSSION QUESTIONS AND ACTIVITIES

Section II. Read chapter 8 (pages 171-194). Discuss your responses to the questions and activities with a classmate. Then write your answers separately.

1. **Why does Stacey say, "This here thing's between Cassie and Lillian Jean and ain't nobody tellin' nobody nothin' 'bout this" (page 173)? Explain whether or not you agree with him.** Stacey forbids his little brothers to tell Mama about the way Cassie is flattering Lillian Jean because he suspects that Cassie has a plan to get back at Lillian Jean for what happened in Strawberry. Stacey realizes that if Cassie's fawning behavior is part of a plan, then she is not guilty of losing her pride, as the younger boys believe. At the same time, if she is planning revenge, it is better to keep the adults out of it. If Mama were aware of Cassie's plan, she would have to either condone it (which would be disastrous for her) or forbid it (which Stacey does not want either). Stacey believes that it is better to trust Cassie to look out for herself and let her act on her own. Answers may vary as to whether students agree with Stacey's reasoning.

2. **What advice does Papa give Cassie about Lillian Jean? Do you think this is good advice? Explain why or why not.** Papa tells Cassie that it is up to her to decide whether or not her problem with Lillian Jean is important enough to her for her to take a stand on it. He also warns her that whatever she decides, she needs to make sure that Charlie Simms will not get involved. This is good advice, because Papa realizes that if Charlie Simms is involved and does something to threaten Cassie or her family, then Papa will be forced to intervene to defend them. If a fight breaks out between Mr. Simms and Papa, there will be serious trouble, and Papa could be killed.

3. **How does Cassie keep Lillian Jean from telling about the fight?** Cassie keeps Lillian Jean from telling about the fight by threatening to reveal all the secrets she has confided to Cassie over the previous month. Cassie also makes sure not to hit or scratch Lillian Jean on the face, so that no one will wonder how she was hurt.

4. **What reasons does Mr. Granger give for Mama losing her teaching job? What do you think the real reason is?** Mr. Granger says that Mama is being fired because she teaches things that are not in the schoolbooks and because she pasted paper over the inside covers of the books. However, the real reason is that Mr. Granger and the Wallaces want to punish the Logans for organizing the boycott of the Wallaces' store. By getting Mama fired, they deprive the family of an important source of income. This puts financial pressure on them and makes it more difficult to pay the taxes and the mortgage. If the Logans fail to make their payments on time, Mr. Granger will have an opportunity to buy back their land.

5. **Why does T.J. tell Kaleb Wallace about what Mama did to the books? What do you think of T.J. for doing this? How does it affect his relationship with the Logan children?** T.J. tells Kaleb Wallace about the books because he is angry with Mama for failing him when she caught him cheating again. Most students will agree that T.J. acted spitefully and with an unconscionable lack of forethought. As usual, he refuses to take responsibility for his own actions, and this time he plays right into the hands of those who want to break the back of the African Americans' resistance to racial injustice. Stacey, who has already twice forgiven T.J. for playing dirty tricks on him (in the first cheat notes incident, and the incident of the wool jacket), has had enough: he will not condone what T.J. has done to Mama. Cassie, Little Man, and even Christopher-John are equally unyielding. After this betrayal, T.J. is no longer their friend in any sense of the word.

Prediction:

What will happen to T.J. in the company of his new white "friends"?

Guided Discussion:

Discuss some of the key questions in Section II. In addition, feel free to include in your discussion questions that are not in the Discussion Guide. Be sure to discuss the questions raised in the Writer's Craft Box on **foreshadowing**. A clue to T.J.'s impending downfall is found at the end of this chapter, when T.J. informs the Logan children that he no longer needs their friendship, since he has other friends "and they white too!" (page 194). Ask students if they remember the general warning Papa gave Stacey about the dangers of friendships between white and black (pages 157-158). While Papa's reticence may have been unwarranted in Jeremy Simms' case, it is probably a valid generalization in the context of 1930s Mississippi. Ask students if they can think of other hints of trouble to come for T.J. They might think of his fascination with the pearl-handled pistol at Barnett's Mercantile in Strawberry (pages 108-109, 155-156). When T.J. first shows Stacey the gun, he says, "I'd sell my life for that gun... I get me that gun and ain't nobody gonna mess with me." Invite students to share their opinions as to whether T.J.'s view of the gun is realistic or not. Where do they think his fixation on it may lead him?

You may also want to ask students why they think Mama's history lesson was different from what was in the textbooks (pages 183-184). The content of Mama's lesson is summarized on page 183. We may guess that the county-supplied textbooks glossed over the cruelty of slavery, presenting it as, at worst, a necessary evil. They may even have suggested that African slaves were "ignorant savages" or "simple, childlike souls" for whom slavery was somehow beneficial. Obviously, Mama would take pains to correct such impressions.

 Prediction Check-up

Return to the vocabulary prediction chart, and use it to check the predictions students made prior to reading this section of the reading selection. Remind students that, even if their predictions did not prove true, the value was in making them.

Selection Review

1. **When the Logan family is gathered for Christmas Eve, there is a *flashback* in which Mr. Morrison tells about a Christmas many years before. What do we learn about Mr. Morrison and his background?** On Christmas Eve, Mr. Morrison tells about a Christmas when he was a small child. Some "night men" attacked his home, burning and slashing with their swords. Mr. Morrison's parents were former slaves bred for size and strength. They fought back as hard as they could, but both they and Mr. Morrison's sisters were killed in the attack. This flashback helps us understand why Mr. Morrison is so determined to fight against racism in every way he can.

2. **Why does Jeremy Simms come to visit Stacey on Christmas Day? Papa advises Stacey not to become friends with Jeremy. What are the good points and bad points of this advice?** Jeremy comes to visit Stacey on Christmas to bring him a gift, a handmade wooden flute, as a sign of his friendship. Papa knows that it can be dangerous for white people and black people to be friends in Mississippi in the 1930s. He is concerned about whether Jeremy's attitude toward Stacey will change as they get older. While Papa's advice is based on what he has seen in his own life, he is probably not being fair to Jeremy. He assumes that Jeremy would not be a good friend just because he is white.

3. **Mr. Jamison and Mr. Granger are both wealthy white men. However, they react very differently to the boycott against the Wallaces' store. Explain how their reactions are different. What does Mr. Granger hope to get out of this situation?** When Mr. Jamison hears about the boycott, he thinks what the Logans are doing is right. He wants to be a part of it, so he offers to back the credit for the African-American families to shop in Vicksburg. He wants to make sure that the Logans do not lose their land in the struggle. He wants the African-American community to have a fair chance. In contrast, when Mr. Granger hears about the boycott he is angry. He says the Logans are "stirring up trouble." He wants to use the situation to take the farm away from them.

4. **How does Cassie trick Lillian Jean?** Cassie pretends to be sorry about talking back to Lillian Jean in Strawberry. She flatters Lillian Jean by calling her "Miz Lillian Jean" and carrying her books. She gets Lillian Jean to tell her all her secrets. After a

month Cassie takes Lillian Jean deep in the woods. She throws Lillian Jean's books on the ground so that Lillian Jean will hit her. Then Cassie beats Lillian Jean. Lillian Jean can't tell her father about the fight because Cassie threatens to tell all her secrets.

5. **Explain how Mama loses her teaching job. What does Mr. Granger hope to get out of this situation?** Mama loses her teaching job after she fails T.J. for cheating again. T.J. is angry and tells Kaleb Wallace that Mama pasted paper over the covers of the schoolbooks. Kaleb Wallace, Mr. Granger, and a member of the school board come to check up on Mama. They find her teaching information that is not in the books. They use this excuse to fire her. However, Mr. Granger really wants to make the Logans stop boycotting the Wallaces' store. Most of all, he hopes they will not be able to make the payments on their land. Then he could get it himself.

 **Literature-Related Writing**

1. Papa says, "Far as I'm concerned, friendship between black and white don't mean that much 'cause it usually ain't on an equal basis... Maybe one day whites and blacks can be real friends, but right now the country ain't built that way" (pages 157-158). What do you think about what Papa said? Do you have a friend of another race? Write a short **essay** responding to Papa's statement. Tell whether you think it is easier for people of different races to be friends now than it was in 1933, when this story takes place. Use an example from your own experience and an example from the book to prove your point.

2. On Christmas Eve, Mr. Morrison shares an important part of his family history with the Logan family. Write a **personal narrative** telling about an important part of your own family history: something that happened when you were a child, or that you have heard about from older relatives, that has shaped the way you look at life.

3. Pretend you are Stacey. Write **journal entries** describing your feelings and reactions to some or all of the following incidents:
   - letting T.J. keep your coat;
   - Jeremy's Christmas gift, and Papa's advice;
   - Cassie playing up to Lillian Jean;
   - Mama losing her teaching job;
   - learning that T.J. "told on" Mama to the Wallaces.

Extension Activities

1. Research Alexander Dumas, the author of *The Three Musketeers* and *The Count of Monte Cristo*. Report what you learn to your class.

2. Jeremy makes Stacey a wooden flute for Christmas. Use Internet or library resources to learn how a wooden flute is made and what makes it work. Share what you learn with your classmates.

3. With some other students, act out the school board's visit to Mama's classroom.

Literature Test

1. **What happened to Mr. Morrison's parents and sisters?** Mr. Morrison's home was attacked and burned by "night men" when he was a small boy. His two sisters died in the fire and his parents were both killed.

2. **List several ways that Jeremy Simms and Mr. Jamison are similar.** Jeremy and Mr. Jamison are both white. Both of them are respectful and friendly toward African Americans. Both of them have the courage to do what they think is right even though other white people may make them suffer for it.

3. **Why is Lillian Jean surprised when Cassie beats her?** Lillian Jean is surprised because Cassie spent a month flattering her to gain her trust. She called her "Miz Lillian Jean" and carried her books for her. Lillian Jean thought that Cassie had decided to accept her supposed "inferiority" to white people, and she did not expect Cassie to stand up for her rights any more.

4. **Why does T.J. tell Kaleb Wallace about Mama pasting paper over the inside cover of the schoolbooks? How do Kaleb Wallace and Harlan Granger plan to turn this situation to their own advantage?** T.J. tells Kaleb Wallace about Mama because he is angry that Mama failed him when she found him cheating again. Kaleb Wallace and Mr. Granger use this excuse to get Mama fired from her job. They want to punish the Logans for organizing the boycott against the store. Mr. Granger also hopes that the financial loss to the Logans will give him an opportunity to take their farm.

Discussion Guide #4

Chapters 9 - 12 (pages 195-276)

Vocabulary List A

seeped (p. 195)	*immobilized (p. 211)	curt (p. 231)
vital (p. 196)	*agitated (adj., p. 213)	revival (p. 233)
soberly (p. 197)	despondently (p. 223)	sweltering (p. 234)
persnickety (p. 197)	condemning (p. 224)	*adamantly (p. 237)
caressed (p. 201)	*phenomenal (p. 225)	wistfully (p. 238)
ventured (p. 202)	*frenzied (p. 226)	suffocating (adj., p. 239)
amenities (p. 203)	lethargically (p. 227)	*condescending (adj., p. 240)
chain gang (p. 204)	reproachfully (p. 229)	
exasperation (p. 208)	*persistent (p. 229)	en masse (p. 240)
premature (p. 209)	amber (p. 229)	desolately (p. 241)

Glossary of Starred Words

immobilized - kept from moving

agitated - nervous; upset; disturbed

frenzied - wild; frantic; desperate

phenomenal - amazing; astonishing; incredible

persistent - long-lasting; not stopping

adamantly - firmly; stubbornly; with great determination

condescending - looking down on

Sample Meaningful Sentences for Starred Words

1. When Marvin hurt his ankle, the coach **immobilized** it by wrapping it tightly in a bandage so that it would not move.

2. When Mrs. Delcher realized that her wallet was missing, she became very **agitated**, talking very fast and running her hands wildly through her hair.

3. Mother ran outside screaming and shouting Billy's name in **frenzied** panic, terribly afraid that he would wander into the street and be hit by a car.

4. When the volcano erupted, it sent a **phenomenal** column of smoke and ash shooting five miles straight up in the air, to the amazement of scientists all over the world.

5. The children grew tired of the **persistent** rains that had kept them indoors all the time for over a week.

6. I was hoping that Mom would let me stay up late, but she **adamantly** insisted that I needed to go to bed so that I could wake up early for school the next day.

7. "A third-grader like you could not possibly understand our teenage problems," DeAsia informed her little sister in a **condescending** tone of superiority.

The Writer's Craft

Conflict and *Complication*

The **conflict** in a story is the struggle between the main character or characters and some problem or difficulty. The problem may be internal: a struggle within a character himself. Or it can be external: between the main characters and other characters, nature, or society. **Complications** are additional problems that arise and add to the conflict in the story.

continued on page 51

> When we read *Roll of Thunder, Hear My Cry*, we might think at first that the conflict is between black people and white people. But if we think about it carefully, we realize that it is not that simple. Not all of the white people are bad – and not all of the black people are good. Who or what do you think are the Logan family's real enemies? What complications make their situation even more challenging?

DISCUSSION QUESTIONS AND ACTIVITIES

Section I. Read chapters 9-10 (pages 195-241). Discuss your responses to the questions and activities with a classmate. Then write your answers separately.

1. **List three reasons why Mr. Avery and Mr. Lanier pull out of the shopping boycott. Why doesn't Mama want Papa and Mr. Morrison to go shopping in Vicksburg?** Mr. Avery and Mr. Lanier pull out of the boycott because Mr. Granger and the Wallaces put pressure on them in several ways. First, Mr. Granger decides that the sharecroppers on his property will have to give him sixty percent of their cotton crop instead of fifty as they have been doing. Secondly, he says that if they don't stop shopping in Vicksburg, they will have to move off his land. Finally, Mr. Wallace tells the sharecropping families that he will make them pay off their debts at his store right away or send the sheriff to put them on a chain gang. Mama doesn't want Papa and Mr. Morrison to go shopping in Vicksburg because she is afraid something bad will happen to them. Also, there are only seven families still participating in the boycott, and Mama says this is not enough to really hurt the Wallaces, just annoy them.

2. **Explain why Papa compares the Logans to the fig tree (page 206). What are the similarities? What conclusion does Papa draw?** Papa says that the Logans are like the fig tree because, although the fig tree is not very big, its roots go down deep. Similarly, although the Logans are not as wealthy or powerful as their white neighbors, their "roots" of pride and family tradition

go deep. Like the fig tree, they go on drawing their sustenance from the land and working hard to be productive. Papa's conclusion is that they must never give up, but continue to grow and do what they have to do.

3. **What happened to Papa on the way home from Vicksburg? Do you think Stacey is right to blame himself? Why or why not?** On the way home from Vicksburg, the back wheels of the wagon came off. Papa asked Stacey to hold the mule's reins while he and Mr. Morrison fixed the wheels. However, a truck drove up and some men shot at Papa while he was working. As Papa fell back, Jack reared up, frightened by the shot. The wagon rolled over Papa's leg and broke it. Of course, Stacey is wrong to blame himself for not being able to keep Jack still; he did the best he could. The responsibility for the accident lies with the men who caused it, by tampering with the wheels and by shooting at Papa.

4. **Why does Jeremy spend time in the forest with the Logan children? Why do they worry about T.J.? Turn to the "Character Portrait" pages for Jeremy and T.J. Add any new traits or supporting evidence you have noticed in these chapters.** Jeremy spends time with the Logans in the forest because he enjoys their company, and he gets lonely at home. Since school is out, he does not see them on the road, and neither his parents nor theirs would approve of the children visiting at each other's homes. The children worry about T.J. because Jeremy reports that he is spending a lot of time with Jeremy's older brothers, R.W. and Melvin, who flatter him when he is present but laugh at him behind his back. In the community, people have reported thefts in their homes after T.J. has been around with his new "friends."

Information that could be added to the "Character Portraits" includes:

Jeremy – [Lonely]: He walks over a mile to spend time with the Logans. He sleeps up in a tree house he made.

T.J. – [Dishonest]: He is becoming involved in theft.

Naïve or gullible: He doesn't realize that the Simms' friendship is not sincere.

[Likes attention]: He brings the Simms boys to a revival hoping to impress everyone with his new clothes and his white friends.

Make A Prediction:

Why do you think the Simms boys are taking T.J. to Strawberry?

5. **Why doesn't Papa want to borrow money from Uncle Hammer? What makes him change his mind? What do we learn from Uncle Hammer's response?** Papa doesn't want to borrow money from Uncle Hammer because he doesn't want Uncle Hammer to find out what the Wallaces did to him. He is afraid Uncle Hammer will lose his temper and do something foolish. However, Papa decides he has to call Uncle Hammer when the bank demands that the Logans pay off the entire mortgage immediately. Uncle Hammer responds immediately, borrowing some money and selling his car so that he can pay the debt. His reaction shows us that Uncle Hammer has a clear sense of priorities and is willing to make great sacrifices for the good of the family.

Guided Discussion:

Discuss some of the key questions and activities in Section I. In addition, feel free to include in your discussion questions that are not in the Discussion Guide. Be sure to discuss the questions raised in the Writer's Craft Box on "Conflict and Complication." Obviously, the Logans' enemies include Harlan Granger and the Wallaces. More importantly, however, they are fighting a social system of racial injustice, which gives Granger and the Wallaces all the advantages in the conflict. Ask students to list different types of pressure that have been applied to those involved in the boycott. These should include the following facts:

- Mama was fired from her teaching job;

- the sharecropping families were required to give landowners a higher percentage of their crop;

- sharecroppers would be evicted from their land if they continued the boycott;

- those with debts at the Wallaces' store were threatened with the chain gang;

- Papa was shot and his leg broken, so he could not work on the railroad;

- the bank called in the Logans' mortgage even though they had four more years to pay it.

continued on page 54

> In a sense, all of these actions could be considered complications in the larger conflict that pits the Logans against the system. In addition, as we shall see, T.J.'s foolish, irresponsible behavior will lead to yet another devastating complication in the African-American community's struggle for dignity and justice.

 **Prediction Check-up**

Return to the vocabulary prediction chart, and use it to check the predictions students made prior to reading this section of the reading selection. Remind students that, even if their predictions did not prove true, the value was in making them.

Vocabulary List B

recitation (p. 243)   frantically (p. 249)   welling (p. 255)
grimaced (p. 244)   prone (p. 253)   *affirmation (p. 255)
despicable (p. 249) crescendo (p. 254)   transfixed (adj., p. 263)
*vulnerability (p. 249)

> **Glossary of Starred Words**
>
> **vulnerability** - weakness; helplessness
>
> **affirmation** - statement; agreement

Sample Meaningful Sentences for Starred Words

1. When the cat saw the baby bird lying helplessly on the ground, she took advantage of its **vulnerability** and pounced on it at once.

2. John's testimony about the way Wendell had helped him out was an **affirmation** of my own belief in Wendell's kindness and good will.

# The Writer's Craft

Climax and *Denouement*

The **climax** of a story is the point at which the conflict comes to a head, leading to a resolution. What is the climax of *Roll of Thunder, Hear My Cry*?

The word **denouement** (day-noo-MANH) refers to the resolution of the conflict, the "falling into place" of the different bits of the story after the climax. What is the surprising denouement here? Are there things you still wonder about?

DISCUSSION QUESTIONS AND ACTIVITIES

Section II. Read chapters 11 and 12 (pages 242-276). Discuss your responses to the questions and activities with a classmate. Then write your answers separately.

1. **Why is T.J. frightened? Why do you think Stacey feels responsible for T.J.?** T.J. is frightened because R.W. and Melvin tricked him into helping them break into Mr. Barnett's store in Strawberry. When Mr. Barnett discovered them, they hit him in the head and knocked his wife to the ground. They left both of them unconscious, then beat T.J. savagely when he threatened to tell people that they were the ones who broke into the store. T.J. is badly hurt and very afraid of what will happen to him if anyone finds out that he was involved. Stacey feels responsible for T.J. because he is the only person who has ever been T.J.'s friend. He may also feel responsible since T.J. got involved with the Simms after Stacey withdrew his friendship from him.

2. **Explain why R.W. and Melvin are with the night men accusing T.J. of the robbery. What do the men want to do with the "three new ropes"?** R.W. and Melvin are with the night men because they claim to have seen T.J. running from the store with two other African Americans. Mrs. Barnett believed that all three of the robbers were black because the Simms boys wore

dark stockings over their heads. R.W. and Melvin intend to put all of the blame for the robbery on T.J., since no one will believe his word against theirs. The men plan to lynch T.J., and they decide to hang Mr. Morrison and Papa too while they are at it.

3. **How do Mr. Jamison and the sheriff try to stop the lynching? Why do you think Mr. Granger doesn't do anything to stop the men, even though he says he doesn't want a hanging on his property?** Mr. Jamison and the sheriff try to get the men to let them take T.J. to Strawberry, where he can stand trial. Mr. Granger doesn't want the men to take the law into their own hands on his property, perhaps because it undermines his feeling of being in charge; yet he doesn't really do anything to stop them. Perhaps he secretly thinks a lynching might be just what is needed to "put the colored people in their place."

4. **How does Papa force Mr. Granger to step in and stop the lynching? Why do all the men join together to help Papa and Mr. Morrison put out the fire in the cotton field?** Papa forces Mr. Granger to intervene by setting fire to the Logan cotton field. The wind is blowing the fire toward Mr. Granger's trees, so Mr. Granger makes the men stop the lynching and come help put the fire out. The men all work together to stop the fire because they know that the forest is very dry, and if the fire reaches there, it could burn "all the way to Strawberry."

5. **Give two reasons why the weather is important in the success of Papa's plan to stop the lynching. What risks does he take in setting the cotton field on fire? What do we learn here about Papa's character?** The weather is important for two reasons. First, there have been lightning strikes all evening, and Papa is counting on the fact that people will assume that the fire was started by lightning and not suspect that he did it himself. Secondly, the fire spreads widely enough that it is almost out of control, even with all the men and Mama and Big Ma trying to put it out. They only get control of it after the rain finally starts to fall. Papa takes several risks when he sets the cotton field on fire. One is the very high probability that a large part of the crop will be destroyed and he will not have enough money to pay the taxes. Another is the risk that the fire will indeed get out of control and burn not only the cotton, but also the trees. Finally, there is the risk that Papa's role in setting the fire might be suspected.

Papa's willingness to take these risks says much about his character. He is a man of great courage and decisive action, willing to do what needs to be done and to face the consequences. He also takes all these risks to rescue T.J., even though he has every reason to bear a grudge against T.J. for his role in Mama's firing. Obviously Papa is a man who is not vindictive and who is willing to protect those who hardly deserve it and who cannot take care of themselves.

Guided Discussion:

Discuss some of the key questions in Section II. In addition, feel free to include in your discussion questions that are not in the Discussion Guide. Be sure to address the questions raised in the Writer's Craft Box entitled **Climax and Denouement.** The climax of the book comes when Cassie and her siblings realize that the night men are getting ready to come and lynch Papa and Mr. Morrison as well as T.J. Their report at home sends Papa out to bring about a surprising resolution: ending one crisis by creating another. Significantly, however, the story does not have a neat, simplistic, "happily ever after" type of ending. You might want to ask students whether in their opinion the book has a happy or a sad ending, and to support their positions. Make a T-chart like the one below to list the good and bad points of the ending:

Things That Make the Ending a Sad One	Things That Make the Ending a Good One
A quarter of the cotton is burned up.	The lynching was stopped.
The Logans' future is still uncertain.	The fire was stopped before it destroyed the trees.
Mr. Barnett has died, and T.J. could still be executed for his murder.	The Logans still have their land and their dignity, as well as the determination to do what is necessary to keep both.

continued on page 58

Ask students why they think the story ends with Cassie crying, "for T.J. and the land." While there is a note of hope in the story's ending, it is also a tragic one. Although Cassie has never liked T.J., she realizes that his weakness of character has made him a victim of a situation that is tragically unjust. She cries because he will probably be found guilty of a crime he did not commit, and there is nothing anyone can do to save him from the fate determined for him by a legal system where all the cards will be stacked against him. She also cries because in order to stop the worst injustice – lynching – Papa has had to sacrifice, if only partially and temporarily, that which is most precious to him, the family farm.

Ask students why they think Mildred Taylor ends the story as she does. Answers will vary; however, it seems clear that the writer wants to make the point that there was no quick, easy victory for African Americans dealing with a system so deeply rooted in racial injustice. Every gain, however slight, was made at the cost of great sacrifice and risk, and there were no guarantees for the future.

Finally, ask students what the novel's title means to them now that they have finished reading it. Of course, it is drawn from the song Mr. Morrison sang as he watched over the farm, a song of determination to survive and to resist. On another level, in the final chapters of the novel the thunder broods over the countryside throughout the night of terror and violence. As the characters struggle to contain the fire and prevent widespread devastation to the entire area, the rain finally begins to fall, making it possible for their efforts to succeed. The struggle against the fire can be understood as symbolic of the much larger struggle throughout the novel to combat racial hatred and injustice. Like the fire, this hatred threatens the welfare of the whole community, and the whole community must come together in the effort to eradicate it. (It is interesting that it is Jeremy Simms who begins to dance for joy when the rain finally comes.) In this view, the words "Roll of thunder, hear my cry" might be seen as symbolic of a prayer for the assistance of a higher power

continued on page 59

> to come to the aid of those who have done all they could to help themselves. The system of hatred and injustice was out of control, and some greater intervention would be necessary to overcome it. This implication seems almost inescapably suggestive of the struggles, sacrifices, and cataclysmic forces involved in the Civil Rights movement of the late 1950s and early 1960s.

 **Prediction Check-up**

Return to the vocabulary prediction chart, and use it to check the predictions students made prior to reading this section of the reading selection. Remind students that, even if their predictions did not prove true, the value was in making them.

 Selection Review

1. **List several ways Mr. Granger and the Wallaces put pressure on the sharecroppers to stop boycotting the store.** Mr. Granger and the Wallaces apply pressure on the sharecroppers in three ways. First, Mr. Granger requires the sharecroppers to give him 60% of their cotton crop, instead of 50% as they have in the past. Second, Mr. Granger threatens to put the sharecroppers out of their homes if they continue the boycott. Third, the Wallaces tell those that have debts at the store that they must pay off their debts immediately or the sheriff will arrest them and put them to work on the chain gang.

2. **Why do the Logans have a hard time making ends meet financially? How does Uncle Hammer come to their rescue?** After Mama lost her teaching job, the Logans counted on Papa's railroad job for the mortgage money. However, the Wallaces attack the wagon as Papa, Stacey, and Mr. Morrison are coming home from Vicksburg. Papa is wounded in the head and his leg is broken, so he cannot work on the railroad. In the summer, the bank calls in the Logans' mortgage, even though they were

supposed to have four more years to pay it off. Uncle Hammer sells his Packard and borrows some money so that the mortgage can be paid off.

3. **What do the Logan children learn about T.J. from Jeremy Simms and other neighbors?** Jeremy tells the children that T.J. spends a lot of time with Jeremy's older brothers, R.W. and Melvin. Jeremy is angry because his brothers pretend to like T.J., but make fun of him behind his back. The children are also concerned because some of the neighbors report things being stolen when T.J. and his new friends visit them.

4. **Why do the night men come after T.J.? Why does Stacey send Cassie and the younger boys to get Papa and Mr. Morrison?** T.J. helped the Simms boys break into Barnett's store in Strawberry. When Mr. Barnett discovered them, they hit him on they head and knocked his wife on the ground. The Simms boys were wearing dark stockings over their faces, so Mrs. Barnett thought they were black. Later, the Simms boys pretend they had nothing to do with the crime. They say they saw T.J. and two other black boys running away from the store. They come with the night men to lynch T.J. They threaten to hang Papa and Mr. Morrison as well. Stacey sends the younger children home to get Papa and Mr. Morrison before the men hurt T.J. any more.

5. **How does Papa plan to make Mr. Granger stop the lynching? How successful is his plan?** Papa plans to make Mr. Granger stop the lynching by setting the cotton on fire. He expects that people will think that lightning started the fire, and he knows the wind will carry the fire toward Mr. Granger's trees. Mr. Granger will make the men stop the lynching so that they can fight the fire. Papa's plan succeeds in stopping the lynching. However, a quarter of the cotton crop is burned up. It will be hard for the Logans to find the money to pay the taxes. T.J. is saved from lynching, but Mr. Barnett dies during the night. T.J. will have to stand trial for murder. He could still go on the chain gang or even be killed.

Literature-Related Writing

1. What do you think Jeremy Simms thinks about up in his tree house? Pretend you are Jeremy. Write several **journal entries** from his point of view about the events recounted in these chapters.

2. Pretend you are Wade Jamison. You are going to defend T.J. at his trial for the murder of Mr. Barnett. Write an **opening statement** in which you lay out arguments and evidence for your position that T.J. is innocent of the crime. (Remember, a Mississippi jury in 1933 will not believe T.J.'s word against that of R.W. and Melvin. You will have to find other arguments to convince them.)

3. With a quarter of the cotton crop destroyed, how do you think the Logans will raise the money they need to live on and pay the taxes? Write a **short story** about what the Logans will do next in order to survive.

Extension Activities

1. Make a map of the setting of these chapters, from the Logans' farm on out to Strawberry.

2. Draw or paint a picture to illustrate a scene from this part of the book.

3. With other students, act out a dramatic scene from the book for your class.

Literature Test

1. **Why do most of the sharecroppers pull out of the shopping boycott?** Most of the sharecroppers pull out of the boycott because the landowners decide to take 60% of the cotton crop from them instead of 50%. Mr. Granger threatens to evict them from their homes. The Wallaces threaten those that have debts at the store that they will be put on the chain gang to pay off their debts.

2. **List the reasons for the Logans' financial difficulties. Explain why Uncle Hammer sells his car.** The Logans have financial trouble because Mama lost her teaching job and the Wallaces attacked Papa on the road, shooting him in the head and causing his leg to be broken so he could not work for the railroad. Also, the bank called in the mortgage, even though the Logans were supposed to have four more years to pay it. Uncle Hammer sells his car to get the money to pay off the mortgage.

3. **How does T.J. get in trouble? Why are the Simms boys not blamed for the break-in?** T.J. gets in trouble by helping the Simms break into the Barnetts' store. The boys knock the Barnetts down and leave them unconscious on the floor. They beat T.J. savagely, then later claim they saw him running from the store with two other black boys. The Simms are not blamed because they covered their faces with dark stockings.

4. **What does Papa sacrifice in order to make Mr. Granger stop the lynching? Why is Cassie sad at the end of the novel?** Papa sets fire to his cotton field to make Mr. Granger stop the lynching. Cassie is sad partly because of the damage to the land, but mostly because T.J. will have to stand trial for Mr. Barnett's murder. He will probably be sentenced to death or the chain gang in spite of all Papa's efforts.

TEACHER'S MANUAL | 63
Black Line Master for Transparencies

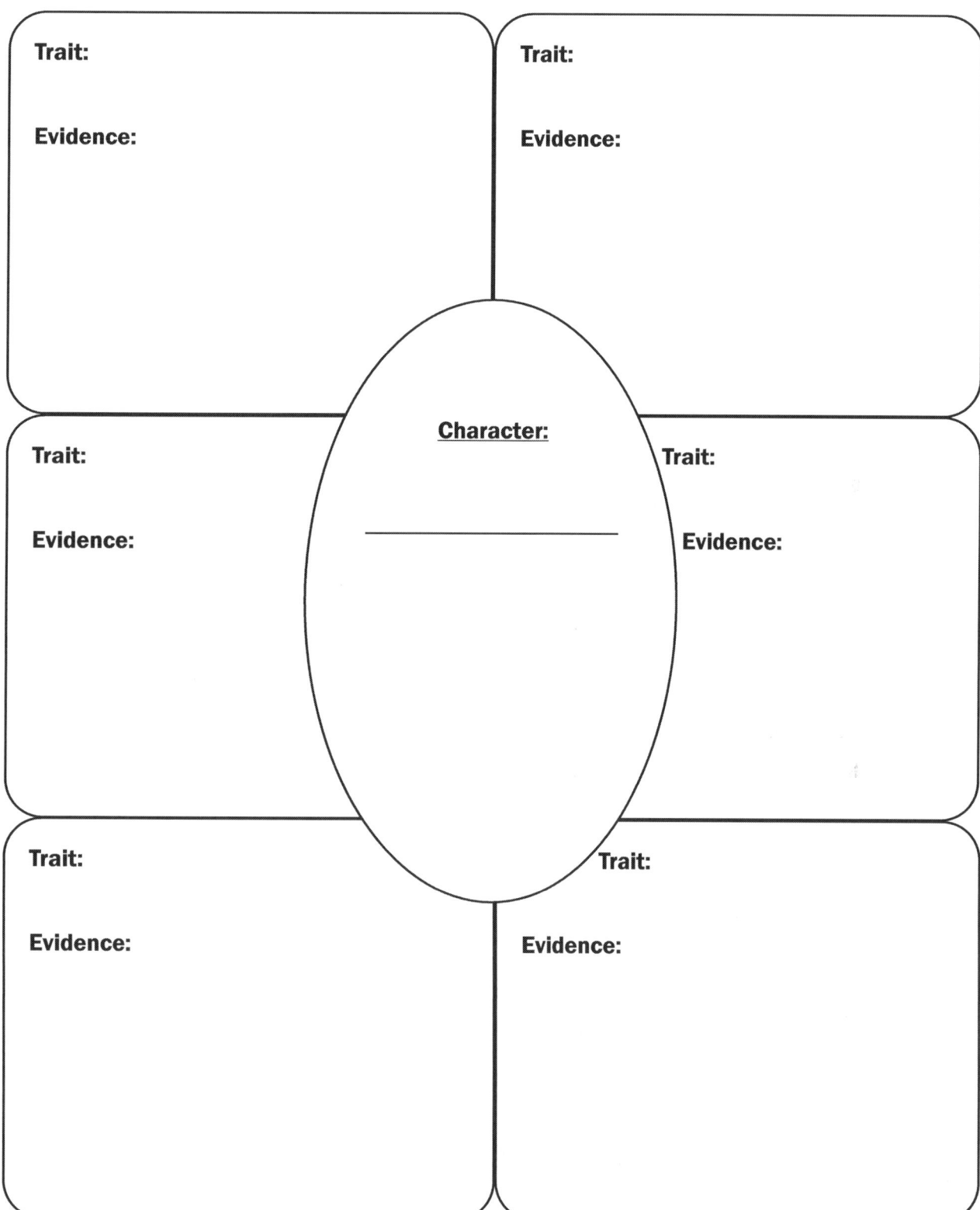

Talent Development Secondary Program

Selection Review #1

Roll of Thunder, Hear My Cry

Chapters 1-3

1. **List some of the reasons that Cassie, Christopher-John, and Little Man dislike T.J.** The children dislike T.J. because he is dishonest. He wants Stacey to help him cheat at school. He is also mean. Instead of taking his punishment, he lies so that his mother will punish his little brother Claude instead. He laughs at Little Man when his clothes get dirty. T.J. also makes the children angry by teasing them with tidbits of gossip.

2. **Why do Cassie and Little Man get in trouble the first day of school? How does Mama show that she agrees with them?** Cassie and Little Man get in trouble on the first day of school because they do not want their "new" school textbooks. Little Man does not want his book at first because it is old, dirty, and in poor condition. When he takes the book anyway, he finds insulting words about the students' race written on the inside cover. He throws the book on the floor and jumps on it. When Cassie tries to explain to Miss Crocker why Little Man is angry, Miss Crocker becomes angry with both children. However, when Miss Crocker reports their behavior to Mama, Mama pastes paper over the inside cover. Cassie realizes that Mama understands why the children were angry.

3. **Why is Papa concerned about the family's safety? What does he do to try to protect them?** Papa is concerned about the family's safety because some white men set fire to three African Americans, killing one of them. Papa takes two safety measures to protect the family. He asks his friend, Mr. Morrison, to stay with them while he is away working for the railroad. Mr. Morrison is a huge, powerful man. Papa hopes that he will be able to keep danger away. Papa also strictly warns the children to stay away from the Wallaces' store. He is afraid that some day there will be serious trouble for the young people who spend time there.

4. **Describe two ways the children express their anger after the bus soaks them with mud. Which reaction do you think was fairer?** After the bus splashes them, the children express their anger by being unfriendly to Jeremy. They also express their anger by digging a big ditch in the road. The Jefferson Davis bus breaks down and the white children have to walk home. Although this causes a lot of trouble, in a way it is fairer, because it punishes the people who caused the problem. The bus driver and the white children who laughed find out how it feels to walk home soaked with mud. They also have to walk to school every day for several weeks. On the other hand, being unfriendly to Jeremy is not fair. In their anger, the children are hurting someone who tries to be nice to them. Jeremy had nothing to do with the problem. He never even rides the bus.

continued...

5. **Why do the children feel frightened and guilty when they hear that the white men are going to make trouble again?** The children are frightened when they hear that the white men plan to make trouble because they think that the men are angry with them for making the bus break down. They are especially frightened because they know that white men set the Berry men on fire. They wonder whether they will be burned up too. The children, especially Stacey, feel guilty because they think they have brought more trouble to their community.

Selection Review #2

Roll of Thunder, Hear My Cry

Chapters 4-6

1. **What are some ways Stacey could have solved his problem with T.J. *without* going to the Wallaces' store?** There are several ways that Stacey could have handled this situation differently. He could have told Mama the truth about where he got the answers for the history test. He could have taken T.J.'s punishment, but later told T.J. that they could not be friends unless T.J. told Mama the truth. Stacey could also have waited to deal with T.J. when he came home from the store.

2. **Why is Cassie's grandmother determined not to sell the family farm to Mr. Granger?** A Yankee bought a big piece of the Granger plantation after the Civil War. Cassie's grandfather, Paul Edward Logan, bought the first 200 acres from him. He paid off the mortgage and tried to buy more land. The younger Mr. Jamison finally sold him another 200 acres. Big Ma refuses to sell the land because she and her husband worked very hard to get it and keep it. It holds precious memories for her. It is the heritage Paul Edward left for her and her two living sons, Papa and Uncle Hammer.

3. **How does Mama make the children understand that the Wallaces are bad people? What does she want the African-American families to do to fight against the Wallaces' bad influence?** Mama takes the children to visit Mr. Berry. He is one of the men that the Wallaces set on fire. He is suffering terribly and hardly even looks like a human being. Mama wants the African-American families to keep their children away from the Wallaces' store. She also asks them to stop shopping there. She offers to help them get credit to shop in Vicksburg.

4. **Why does Cassie have a terrible day when she goes to Strawberry with Big Ma?** Cassie finds out in Strawberry how unfairly some white people treat African Americans. She is upset that Big Ma has to park her wagon at the back of the field. She becomes angry with Mr. Barnett, the storekeeper. He keeps her, Stacey, and T.J. waiting for a long time while he fills orders for white people. Finally, when Cassie bumps into Lillian Jean by accident, she has to apologize to her. Lillian Jean's father grabs Cassie's arm and knocks her down off the sidewalk. He forces Big Ma to make Cassie apologize again, calling Lillian Jean "Miz Lillian Jean."

continued...

5. **Mama and Uncle Hammer have different ways of fighting back against racism. Explain how their ways are different. Which way do you think is better?** Mama wants to fight against racism by getting the African-American community to work together. She wants them to show their feelings about bad treatment by not shopping at the Wallaces' store. Her way is non-violent. Uncle Hammer's way of fighting back is violent. He is ready to act alone. He does not think about the consequences. Uncle Hammer's way is dangerous. It does not give people an opportunity to change. If Uncle Hammer really hurt a white person or burned something down, he would probably be killed. This would be bad for the entire family and the community. Mama's way is slower, but it has a better chance of having some effect.

Selection Review #3

Roll of Thunder, Hear My Cry

Chapters 7 and 8

1. **When the Logan family is gathered for Christmas Eve, there is a *flashback* in which Mr. Morrison tells about a Christmas many years before. What do we learn about Mr. Morrison and his background?** On Christmas Eve, Mr. Morrison tells about a Christmas when he was a small child. Some "night men" attacked his home, burning and slashing with their swords. Mr. Morrison's parents were former slaves bred for size and strength. They fought back as hard as they could, but both they and Mr. Morrison's sisters were killed in the attack. This flashback helps us understand why Mr. Morrison is so determined to fight against racism in every way he can.

2. **Why does Jeremy Simms come to visit Stacey on Christmas Day? Papa advises Stacey not to become friends with Jeremy. What are the good points and bad points of this advice?** Jeremy comes to visit Stacey on Christmas to bring him a gift, a hand-made wooden flute, as a sign of his friendship. Papa knows that it can be dangerous for white people and black people to be friends in Mississippi in the 1930s. He is concerned about whether Jeremy's attitude toward Stacey will change as they get older. While Papa's advice is based on what he has seen in his own life, he is probably not being fair to Jeremy. He assumes that Jeremy would not be a good friend just because he is white.

3. **Mr. Jamison and Mr. Granger are both wealthy white men. However, they react very differently to the boycott against the Wallaces' store. Explain how their reactions are different. What does Mr. Granger hope to get out of this situation?** When Mr. Jamison hears about the boycott, he thinks what the Logans are doing is right. He wants to be a part of it, so he offers to back the credit for the African-American families to shop in Vicksburg. He wants to make sure that the Logans do not lose their land in the struggle. He wants the African-American community to have a fair chance. In contrast, when Mr. Granger hears about the boycott he is angry. He says the Logans are "stirring up trouble." He wants to use the situation to take the farm away from them.

4. **How does Cassie trick Lillian Jean?** Cassie pretends to be sorry about talking back to Lillian Jean in Strawberry. She flatters Lillian Jean by calling her "Miz Lillian Jean" and carrying her books. She gets Lillian Jean to tell her all her secrets. After a month Cassie takes Lillian Jean deep in the woods. She throws Lillian Jean's books on the ground so that Lillian Jean will hit her. Then Cassie beats Lillian Jean. Lillian Jean can't tell her father about the fight because Cassie threatens to tell all her secrets.

continued...

5. Explain how Mama loses her teaching job. What does Mr. Granger hope to get out of this situation? Mama loses her teaching job after she fails T.J. for cheating again. T.J. is angry and tells Kaleb Wallace that Mama pasted paper over the covers of the schoolbooks. Kaleb Wallace, Mr. Granger, and a member of the school board come to check up on Mama. They find her teaching information that is not in the books. They use this excuse to fire her. However, Mr. Granger really wants to make the Logans stop boycotting the Wallaces' store. Most of all, he hopes they will not be able to make the payments on their land. Then he could get it himself.

Selection Review #4

Roll of Thunder, Hear My Cry

Chapters 9-12

1. **List several ways Mr. Granger and the Wallaces put pressure on the sharecroppers to stop boycotting the store.** Mr. Granger and the Wallaces apply pressure on the sharecroppers in three ways. First, Mr. Granger requires the sharecroppers to give him 60% of their cotton crop, instead of 50% as they have in the past. Second, Mr. Granger threatens to put the sharecroppers out of their homes if they continue the boycott. Third, the Wallaces tell those that have debts at the store that they must pay off their debts immediately or the sheriff will arrest them and put them to work on the chain gang.

2. **Why do the Logans have a hard time making ends meet financially? How does Uncle Hammer come to their rescue?** After Mama lost her teaching job, the Logans counted on Papa's railroad job for the mortgage money. However, the Wallaces attack the wagon as Papa, Stacey, and Mr. Morrison are coming home from Vicksburg. Papa is wounded in the head and his leg is broken, so he cannot work on the railroad. In the summer, the bank calls in the Logans' mortgage, even though they were supposed to have four more years to pay it off. Uncle Hammer sells his Packard and borrows some money so that the mortgage can be paid off.

3. **What do the Logan children learn about T.J. from Jeremy Simms and other neighbors?** Jeremy tells the children that T.J. spends a lot of time with Jeremy's older brothers, R.W. and Melvin. Jeremy is angry because his brothers pretend to like T.J., but make fun of him behind his back. The children are also concerned because some of the neighbors report things being stolen when T.J. and his new friends visit them.

4. **Why do the night men come after T.J.? Why does Stacey send Cassie and the younger boys to get Papa and Mr. Morrison?** T.J. helped the Simms boys break into Barnett's store in Strawberry. When Mr. Barnett discovered them, they hit him on they head and knocked his wife on the ground. The Simms boys were wearing dark stockings over their faces, so Mrs. Barnett thought they were black. Later, the Simms boys pretend they had nothing to do with the crime. They say they saw T.J. and two other black boys running away from the store. They come with the night men to lynch T.J. They threaten to hang Papa and Mr. Morrison as well. Stacey sends the younger children home to get Papa and Mr. Morrison before the men hurt T.J. any more.

continued...

5. How does Papa plan to make Mr. Granger stop the lynching? How successful is his plan? Papa plans to make Mr. Granger stop the lynching by setting the cotton on fire. He expects that people will think that lightning started the fire, and he knows the wind will carry the fire toward Mr. Granger's trees. Mr. Granger will make the men stop the lynching so that they can fight the fire. Papa's plan succeeds in stopping the lynching. However, a quarter of the cotton crop is burned up. It will be hard for the Logans to find the money to pay the taxes. T.J. is saved from lynching, but Mr. Barnett dies during the night. T.J. will have to stand trial for murder. He could still go on the chain gang or even be killed.

Name: _____

Literature Test #1

Roll of Thunder, Hear My Cry

Chapters 1–3

1. Tell why you think T.J. would not be a very good friend, giving examples from the story.

   _____
   _____
   _____
   _____
   _____
   _____
   _____

2. Explain why Cassie and Little Man refuse to take their "new" textbooks. How does Mama's reaction to their "misbehavior" differ from Miss Crocker's?

   _____
   _____
   _____
   _____
   _____
   _____
   _____

continued...

3. Why does Papa bring Mr. Morrison to stay with the family? Why does he warn the children to stay away from the Wallaces' store?

4. The evening after they dig a ditch to make the white children's school bus break down, the Logan children are so excited and proud that they cannot stop giggling. What happens to make their feelings change to fear and guilt?

Name: _____

Literature Test #2

Roll of Thunder, Hear My Cry

Chapters 4-6

1. Explain why Stacey gets in trouble at school.

   _____
   _____
   _____
   _____
   _____
   _____
   _____

2. Why does Mama consider the Wallaces bad people? How does she want the African-American community to fight back against them?

   _____
   _____
   _____
   _____
   _____
   _____
   _____

continued...

3. WCassie says of her day in Strawberry, "No day in all my life had ever been as cruel as this one." Why does she say this? What happened that day?

_____

_____

_____

_____

_____

_____

_____

4. How does Uncle Hammer react to the news that Mr. Simms knocked Cassie down? Why do Mama, Big Ma, and Mr. Morrison try to keep Uncle Hammer from going to the Simms' house?

_____

_____

_____

_____

_____

_____

_____

Name: _____

Literature Test #3

Roll of Thunder, Hear My Cry

Chapters 7 and 8

1. When the Logan family is gathered for Christmas Eve, there is a *flashback* in which Mr. Morrison tells about a Christmas many years before. What do we learn about Mr. Morrison and his background?

   _____
   _____
   _____
   _____
   _____
   _____
   _____

2. Why does Jeremy Simms come to visit Stacey on Christmas Day? Papa advises Stacey not to become friends with Jeremy. What are the good points and bad points of this advice?

   _____
   _____
   _____
   _____
   _____
   _____
   _____

continued...

3. Mr. Jamison and Mr. Granger are both wealthy white men. However, they react very differently to the boycott against the Wallaces' store. Explain how their reactions are different. What does Mr. Granger hope to get out of this situation?

4. How does Cassie trick Lillian Jean?

5. Explain how Mama loses her teaching job. What does Mr. Granger hope to get out of this situation?

Name: _____

Literature Test #4

Roll of Thunder, Hear My Cry

Chapters 9-12

1. Why do most of the sharecroppers pull out of the shopping boycott?

   _____
   _____
   _____
   _____
   _____
   _____

2. List the reasons for the Logans' financial difficulties. Explain why Uncle Hammer sells his car.

   _____
   _____
   _____
   _____
   _____
   _____
   _____
   _____

continued...

3. How does T.J. get in trouble? Why are the Simms boys not blamed for the break-in?

4. What does Papa sacrifice in order to make Mr. Granger stop the lynching? Why is Cassie sad at the end of the novel?

Name: _____

Vocabulary Test #1

Roll of Thunder, Hear My Cry

Chapters 1-3

WRITE SENTENCES FOR THE FOLLOWING WORDS:

concession	audible	inaccessible
emblem	indignant	relent
monotonously	dismayed	oblivious
	endured	

_____

_____

_____

_____

_____

_____

_____

_____

_____

_____

_____

_____

Name: _____

Vocabulary Test #2

Roll of Thunder, Hear My Cry

Chapters 4-6

WRITE SENTENCES FOR THE FOLLOWING WORDS:

prevailed	subtle	retaliated
discreetly	patronize	ominously
engrossed	subdued	resigned

Vocabulary Test #3

Roll of Thunder, Hear My Cry

Chapters 7 and 8

WRITE SENTENCES FOR THE FOLLOWING WORDS:

apprehensive	lingered	denote
interminable	acknowledged	condoned
restrained	candidly	morosely
	boycott	

Name: _____

Vocabulary Test #4

Roll of Thunder, Hear My Cry

Chapters 9-12

WRITE SENTENCES FOR THE FOLLOWING WORDS:

immobilized	phenomenal	condescending
agitated	persistent	vulnerability
frenzied	adamantly	affirmation

Student Team Literature Discussion Guides are available for the following titles:

Non-fiction

- The Acorn People
- Anne Frank: The Diary of a Young Girl
- Barack Obama: President for a New Era
- Barack Obama: United States President
- The Double Life of Pocahontas
- First They Killed My Father
- Freedom Train
- Freedom's Children
- Leon's Story
- One More River to Cross: the Stories of Twelve Black Americans
- Warriors Don't Cry
- We Beat the Street
- What's the Big Idea, Ben Franklin?

Short Stories, Poetry, and Mythology

- Beowulf: A New Telling
- The Dark-Thirty: Southern Tales of the Supernatural
- A Dime a Dozen
- The Dream Keeper and Other Poems
- ego-tripping and other poems for young people
- Keeping the Night Watch
- The Library Card
- Locomotion
- Make Lemonade
- The Odyssey, retold by Robin Lister

Novels

- The Big Wave
- Bridge to Terabithia
- Bud, Not Buddy
- The Bully
- Call It Courage
- The Call of the Wild
- The Cay
- Crash
- Curse of a Winter Moon
- Darnell Rock Reporting
- A Day No Pigs Would Die
- Eddie's Ordeal
- Esperanza Rising
- Fast Sam, Cool Clyde, and Stuff
- Freak the Mighty
- The Giver
- Hatchet
- The Hobbit
- Holes
- In the Night, on Lanvale Street
- Jacob Have I Loved
- Johnny Tremain
- Journey
- Justin and the Best Biscuits in the World
- M. C. Higgins the Great
- Maniac Magee
- The Midwife's Apprentice
- Monster
- The Mystery of Apartment A-13
- Ninjas, Piranhas, and Galileo
- Nothing But the Truth
- Number the Stars
- The Outsiders
- The Pinballs
- Roll of Thunder, Hear My Cry
- Sing Down the Moon
- The Skin I'm In
- To Kill a Mockingbird
- Touching Spirit Bear
- Tuck Everlasting
- The Watsons Go to Birmingham—1963
- The Westing Game
- The Whipping Boy
- Wringer
- A Wrinkle in Time
- Yolonda's Genius

For a catalog and ordering information, call 410-516-4339
For information on Student Team Literature professional development,
call Maria Waltemeyer (410-516-2247)
or visit the Talent Development Secondary website at
www.talentdevelopmentsecondary.com

Made in the USA
Middletown, DE
03 April 2024

52514326R00053